Marc Reklau

DESTINATION HAPPINESS

12 Simple Principles that will change your life

Disclaimer

This book is designed to provide information and motivation to our readers. It is sold with the understanding that the publisher is not engaged to render any type of psychological, legal, or any other kind of professional advice. The instructions and advice in this book are not intended as a substitute for counseling. The content of each chapter is the sole expression and opinion of its author. No warranties or guarantees are expressed or implied by the author's and publisher's choice to include any of the content in this volume. Neither the publisher nor the individual author shall be liable for any physical, psychological, emotional, financial, or commercial damages, including, but not limited to, special, incidental, consequential or other damages. Our views and rights are the same:

You must test everything for yourself according to your own situation talents and aspirations

You are responsible for your own decisions, choices, actions, and results.

Marc Reklau

Visit my website at www.marcreklau.com

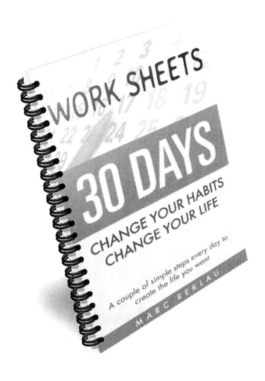

Download your coaching work sheets
www.goodhabitsacademy.com

on my webpage

www.marcreklau.com

If you want to make the world a happier place, start with yourself :)

Contents

Acknowledgements:

Thanks to Natalia Montolio, my partner in life and business, for her constant support, and for brightening my days with her smiles and always-cheerful mood.

Thanks to my family; my mother, Heidi; grandmother, Hilde; my uncle Dieter; and my cousin, Alex and his wife Yvonne (our joint vacations in the beautiful city of Naples, Florida, always inspire me).

Olaf, Paola, Sophie and Adrian for you hospitality in FTL. It's always a pleasure to visit.

My friends Claudio, Christian, Pol, Inma, Oscar and all the new people who came into my life in this amazing last two years.

Stefan Ludwig, my mentor and sounding board for over 15 years.

Big shout out to Jaime Avargues, the first publisher who discovered my first book, '30 DAYS', took a chance and bought the Spanish rights for Latin America even before the book became a bestseller.

Pilar Zaragoza de Pedro, who had the brilliant idea to write a book together, which led to the birth of our own publishing label.

Pilar Cortés García-Moreno, my editor from Planeta. Thank you for believing in me and this new book, and for making my dream of being published by a major publisher come true. It was a long road full of rejections until we met. I'm indeed deeply grateful.

I also want to thank David H. Morgan for his valuable inputs and feedback over the years.

Dr. Steve Mallon, Carlos Moreno Gonzalez, and Lisa Williams for giving me the chance to teach happiness at the Geneva Business school. Also, thanks to Paloma Garcia from GBS and my fabulous bachelor students.

Thank you to my German teacher from high school, Mrs. Gabriele Krohm for believing in me, while your colleague Mr. Scheuthle strongly advised me to not major in German and take Biology instead. Also, thank you to you Mr. Scheuthle for your honesty.

Thank you Angel Miro for applying the Pygmalion Effect with me and making me a better student.

Thanks to everybody who continuously supported me and for believed in me when not a lot of people did.

I also want to thank the people I parted ways with. You were very important to me at one point of time. Things just didn't work out. I appreciate your presence in my life once, and wish you all the best.

But above all, thank you to the following people whose work has had a huge influence on my own work in the last few years, and which, in a lot of ways, made this book possible.

Thanks to Martin Seligman for starting a revolution in Psychology and changing the questions.

To Tal Ben Shahar, for teaching the "Happiness Class" at Harvard University and opening doors for hundreds (or even thousands) of other teachers teaching the subject all over the world.

Shawn Achor, for translating the fantastic studies from the field of Positive Psychology into everyday language that we all can understand.

A huge thank you also goes out to the researchers of the hundreds of studies that provide us with fantastic insights about the power of our mind

And last, but not the least, a HUGE thank you to you, dear readers. Without YOU, this book wouldn't exist. Your e-mails and comments encourage me to continue writing and give me strength in moments of doubts and darkness.

Thank you!

Introduction

I've believed in all the things that I've written about since I was 16 years old. When I started getting into self-help and personal development, most of the things that were taught like "Your Beliefs create your reality" or "You attract what you concentrate on" were mere philosophical concepts that you could believe, or not. There was no scientific basis for it.

However, I still believed.

When I found the science that supports most of the concepts that are introduced in my first book "30 Days– Change your habits, change your life" I became immensely happy, because I knew that thanks to science, I can now even convince the skeptics, at least most of them.

I felt like I was given a superpower, because now – apart from showing that the exercises work by *doing* them – we have science as proof. This, hopefully, will motivate more people to give it a shot. We are quickly running out of the excuses that keep us from doing them.

While 30 Days is primarily a practical book, this book looks more at the scientific side of happiness and the huge impact it has on our life and our potential – at home as well as at work.

The book stems from the classes I taught at the Barcelona Campus of Geneva Business School, which was in most parts, based on my book "30 Days– Change your habits, change your life" and the works of Martin Seligman, Tal Ben Shahar, and Shawn Achor among others. These three men made hundreds of studies in the field of Positive Psychology accessible by "translating" them into a language that everybody could easily understand.

The fact that Tal Ben Shahar taught the "Happiness-class" (Positive Psychology) at Harvard University – which went on to become the most-demanded class at Harvard with over 1,400 students – helped me and hundreds (or even thousands) of other teachers to make this subject an integral part in universities, business schools, and even workplaces– something quite unthinkable till a little over a decade ago.
"Why teach happiness at Harvard?", one may ask. Well, in 2004, the Harvard Crimson Poll found out that 4 in 5 Harvard students suffer from depression at least once during the school year, and nearly half of all

students suffer from continuous depression so debilitating that they can't function. Fast-forward to a couple of years later, these numbers were confirmed by a nationwide study of universities in the U.S.

This book looks at the base question of all questions: How can I become happier?

You will learn how to cultivate the habits and mindset that have been scientifically proven to fuel greater success and fulfillment.

The original formula that my generation and the ones before were taught was the following:

Study hard, get a job, work hard, become successful, and once you are successful, you will be happy. So tell me, my friend, how did that work out for you? For me, it didn't, and when we look around us, we have to admit that this formula obviously doesn't work for most of us.

After more than a decade of research in the fields of Positive Psychology and neuroscience, today we can say that it's actually the other way round: We become more successful when we are happier and optimistic.

Another false concept we were taught was that reaching certain goals fuel happiness. That once when we have the perfect body; once we have a great job; a promotion; a new car; a great house in the most-affluent locality in town; once we have the fattest bank balance; and the worst – once we find the perfect partner – *then*, we will be happy.

But did that work for you? Well, I have good news for you– this too was proven wrong, but worry not, as science also gives the solution of how to find real happiness.

Once again it's not about the information and theory of how to live a happier life.
I want you to use the scientific basis as an additional motivation to apply the material and do the exercises.

But first… why happiness?

Nobody ever teaches us how to find meaning and happiness, and that's why there's lots of trouble in Happiness-Land:

Divorce rates are at 50-60%, and that doesn't mean that the other 40-50% of marriages are just peachy. Because it doesn't include the number of marriages that are intact due to habit, a sense of duty, or due to the fear of change.

Depression rates are ten times higher than it was in the 1960s, and the average onset age of the first depression has dropped from 29.5 years to 14.5 years!

Suicide rates are rising.

Turn on the news and all you see is corruption, murder, terrorism, accidents, war, and abuse. What's worse is that this constant focus on the negative tricks our brain into believing that reality actually looks like this – that most part of life is negative.

Unfortunately, looking at traditional Psychology as late as in the year 1998, the ratio didn't look much better. For every one study on happiness, there were 17 studies on depression and disorder.

And then – thank god – came Martin Seligman, the President of the American Psychological Association, who officially launched the field of Positive Psychology, or the scientific study of optimal human functioning, in 1998.

Seligman concluded that instead of studying what's broken, "we have to study what works." We have to look at what makes some people thrive and succeed even in the most difficult of circumstances. What are successful people doing differently from the others?

We have to focus on what works by looking at the questions we ask because what we focus on creates our reality. So we better start focusing on and cultivating the positive.

And that changed everything…

Being happy is much more than the absence of sadness. Today, thanks to over 200 studies on 275,000 people worldwide, we know that happiness leads to success in nearly every domain of our lives. Being happy improves our health, our marriage, our friendships, our social life, and especially our jobs, careers, and businesses.

It starts with making changes within ourselves. Later on, we can bring the benefits of happiness to our complete environment, such as in our teams, our organizations, and in everyone around us.

The examples and studies shown in this book will bring you proof that happiness and optimism enhance your performance and achievement, providing you with the competitive edge.

Martin Seligman, for example, found out that optimistic salespeople sell a whopping 56% more than their pessimistic counterparts. Further studies show optimism can make CEOs 15% more productive and not only that, they also have healthier teams that perform better. Happy and optimistic managers can improve customer satisfaction by 42%.
And, happy workers have higher levels of productivity, get higher sales figures, perform better in leadership positions, and receive higher work performance ratings.
They are also paid better, and are less likely to take sick leaves.

To summarize, the benefits of happiness are countless. Positive emotions flood our brains with dopamine and serotonin, which make us feel better, make us better at organizing information, and make us able to retain information for longer. We become faster and better creative thinkers. We see new ways of doing things, subsequently making us better at problem-solving.

As I already mentioned, there are countless studies about happiness. One study reveals that the happiness levels in students as freshmen in college predicted how high their income was as much as 19 years later, regardless of their initial level of wealth.

Talking about health. In the famous "Nun-Study" researchers studied the level of positivity in journal entries of nuns and found out that the nuns with joyful and content journal entries lived nearly ten years longer than the ones that were negative or neutral entries. Another study shows that happy employees are healthier and therefore more productive on the job (did we really need a study for that?), but not only that, the Gallup Healthways Wellbeing Index 2008 showed how unhappy employees take more sick leaves, stayed at home 1.25 more days a month than their happy colleagues. This sums up to 15 days a year!

A recent study by the German government shows that employees in Germany missed more workdays due to sickness than in the years before.

How did researchers show the correlation between happiness and health anyway? Easy. They injected people with a cold virus (why didn't we think of this earlier). Happy people felt better at the start of the cold, and even after a week they had fewer symptoms than their unhappy counterparts.
So, let's drill down to what this book really is about.

You have already heard of a lot of things that I've mentioned in this book. I'm not going to tell you anything new. You already know it, and I'm just reminding you.

A lot of times people tell me: "Marc but what you are writing or teaching is common sense!"
And I answer: "Yes it is, but then again common sense is not common action. If it were, we would all be at our ideal weight, working our dream jobs, and living our dream lives, wouldn't we?"

The "Science of Happiness", as Positive Psychology is often called, has built the bridge between the self-help movement with its accessible books, speakers, and workshops, (do phrases like "The 5 steps to a happier life", "3 keys to success" and so on, sound familiar?) but unfortunately, in many cases promise results that are difficult to achieve. On the other hand, we have scientific studies that confirm that these things work, but just very, very few people read them – or can read them. I tried a couple but failed miserably; I just couldn't understand them.

This book, then, is about connecting the best of the two worlds – the scientific studies and the accessibility of self-help.

The important and the most difficult thing is, and I'm not getting tired of repeating this, that it's not the information that determines the quality of your life, it's the application of the information and the putting in practice of the exercises that will make all the difference.

Will this book make a difference in your life? I don't know. If you apply some of the things you learn here, it almost definitely will, and your life will never be the same. Applying these exercises made all the difference in my life. It won't be easy, there will be setbacks and hardships, but it would be worth it.

It's been a bit more than four years since I was fired from my job after being there eleven years. I've made it to best-selling author, with my book read by over 170,000 readers; business school teacher; mentor coach, and I can now earn in a day what I once earned in a month. It was not a walk in the park. It took time, effort, patience, and persistence. There was pain, sadness, doubt, fear, and the temptation to give up numerous times, and above all, a failed marriage, but I kept going on. I hope you do too.

What will you learn after reading this book?

- You'll learn how to overcome for example the fear of failure.
- You'll learn how to overcome perfectionism, which is only debilitating and hurts your progress and peace of mind.
- You'll learn how to improve your relationships

We will look at the importance of gratitude, the importance of physical exercise, and the importance of spending time on relationships and you will read about some mind-boggling studies that hopefully will convince you to give the exercises in this book a shot.

We will look at the importance of perception, interpretation, and focus, which makes all the difference between people that seem to have everything and yet are unhappy and those who enjoy life to the fullest; between those who have nothing and yet never cease to be happy and those who have very little and see themselves as victims of the circumstances

When John Carter studied extraordinary successful people, he found that it came down to only two characteristics that they had, that less successful people didn't have. Only two things mattered, and it wasn't their IQ or their external circumstances, or where they came from.

People who were extraordinary successful had two things in common: firstly they believed in themselves, they believed they are going to make it, and secondly, they kept asking questions. They always wanted to learn.
Please keep just one thing in mind and I will repeat this over and over again: THERE IS NO QUICK FIX.

If you are looking for a quick fix, a magic pill, a proven system that will fix your life in no time, this book is not for you. This stuff works, but it will take some time. Just like how learning to play tennis or any other sport takes some time.

Another warning:

After reading this book, you will NOT be on a constant high and free of pain or succeed in everything you do. That wouldn't be normal. Pain and getting over it, failure and getting up again, ups and downs in life, success and its celebration, victories and losses are all part of life. These are essentials that lead to experiences, learning, and growing.

What you will learn is how to bounce back from hardships quicker, how to deal with failure, how to get over pain faster, and how your focus and your interpretation of events can and will elevate your base level of happiness.

If you don't apply what you learn in this book, it will be just one more book on the shelf.
If you do – this book – or any other about the subject can change your life forever.

Although many people might tell you otherwise, truth remains that THERE IS NO SECRET. The secret, however, if you at all want to look for one, is APPLICATION!

Yes! Happiness can be learned. Resilience can be learned. Bouncing back can be learned. Optimism can be learned. Thanks to neuroscience, we know today that our brain is not a fixed thing. It can actually change.

So how can we become happier and through that, help other individuals, communities, and societies as a whole to become happier? What is happiness and how do you measure it? Is happiness really a destination? Or is it rather a life-long pursuit, or a process of continuous learning?

The first step on the journey is looking within ourselves, introspecting, and making the effort of applying what we learned by introducing behavioral changes in life, which by the way is the only way to bring about real, lasting change.

Are you in? Then let's do this…

1. The Basics

Let's look at the basics, the foundation that we have to lay first, the conditions that have to be in place to begin our journey towards happiness.

1. Applying the science

Good intentions are not enough. We have to take the studies of Positive Psychology and apply them. We need more teachers to know about the Pygmalion effect. They have to know that their expectations are self-fulfilling prophecies, meaning that if they see the greatness in their students, that greatness is much more likely to come alive.

We need more psychologists and doctors to know about the mind-body connection. Who knows about the studies that show that yoga in jail reduces the possibility of second-time offenders? That meditation literally transforms our brain? How many doctors know that 3 x 30 minutes of exercise has the same effect as the most powerful psychiatric drugs?

2. Believing that change is possible

To make changes in your life, first of all, you have to believe that change is possible. But first, here's an interesting question – do genetics matter and if yes, then to what extent?

Lyken and Tellegan, in their famous Minnesota twin study in the 1980s, looked at identical twins that were separated at birth and were brought up and lived in radically different circumstances. The study revealed significant similarities such as:
The twins had wives with the same names, enjoyed drinking the same beer, called their children the same names, had an incredibly similar personality, and similar happiness levels.

They came to the following result: "It may be that trying to be happier is as futile as trying to be taller and is, therefore, counter productive." While this was a very famous quote at the time, it was bad news. **It was also wrong!**

Imagine an unhappy person reading an article like that. He or she's unhappy and reads that we can't become happier, starts believing it, leading it to becoming a self-fulfilling prophecy.

Many years later Lykken said to TIME Magazine. "I made a dumb statement. It is clear that we can change happiness levels, up or down".

There is a lot of evidence that show that people actually do change, for example, through coaching or therapy.
So what happened to Lykken and Tellegen? They made "the error of the average." On an average, when you look at a group of twins, they are just the same.

In reality, many of them are the same, but not all. Those who are not the same are the outliers, and very often it's these outliers that are the most interesting. When researchers started studying the outliers, that's when they got new results.

Genes do matter a lot, science says around 50%, but change is possible! Sometimes it's a sentence or a book that can change your life. We have seen people change as a result of their experiences (PTSD, Post Traumatic Growth – yes, it exists).

So our question shifts from "Is change possible?" to "How is change possible?" and "Why do some individuals succeed despite the circumstances?"

When scientists shifted from studying the average people who hadn't changed to studying the happiest people, they learned that everything changed. When we study what works, when we study the best, that's when we can come to understanding the potential in each one of us.

The Power of One

Unfortunately, we underestimate our power to bring about a change. But yes! One person can make a significant difference. Why? Because all change begins in the mind of a single individual, and then it expands, or as Margaret Mead puts it: "Never doubt that a small group of thoughtful, committed citizens can change the world. In fact it's the only thing that ever will."

We underestimate our capacity to bring a change because we underestimate the potential of the exponential function and change happens exponentially. Think, for example, about the exponential nature of social networks. It's said that within six degrees of separation, we are connected to everyone on this planet.

Or think of smiles. Smiles are contagious. If you make three people smile and these three people each make three other people smile and so on, then within 20 degrees of separation, the whole world would be smiling. The same happens when you make people feel good.

We actually influence people every minute of our life. The only question is: In which direction are we going to do it? Will we be a force for change by applying our knowledge or will we just have good intentions, will we just talk about change without actually putting in the effort?
So yes! Change is possible. It's now proven that we can change our brain through mere practice.

We can rewire our brains to be more positive, creative, resilient, and productive – to see opportunities wherever we turn to look. Our brains can be changed by our thoughts and our daily behavior. We can learn to become happier. Pessimists can learn to become optimists and stressed negative brains can be trained to become relaxed and see more opportunities. But as all training, it takes EFFORT.

Which factors influence our happiness

Most of us think that the influence of external factors on our happiness is huge.

For example, who do you think is happier? People who won the lottery or people who got paralyzed after an accident? This was a groundbreaking study with surprising results...

Yes, the lottery winners were very happy, but not for very long. After six months they went back to their previous levels of happiness. The accident victims were sad, but surprisingly after six months, they went back to their previous levels of happiness.

The same studies were done with professors. They were asked how happy would they be if they got tenure, to which they answered "very happy for the rest of my life." And others were asked how unhappy would they be on not getting tenure and they answered "very unhappy for a very long time." When researchers went back to them three months later, every person had gone back to their previous level of well-being. If they were happy before, they were happy six months later, and if they were unhappy before, they were unhappy six months later. Whether it was the lottery winner, accident victim, or the professor, everybody went back to their base level of happiness. This shows that it's very difficult to change happiness based on external factors, and there's a lot of research supporting this. It also shows that we all gravitate around a base level of happiness. The goal then becomes to raise this base level, and it can be done with the exercises I'm going to mention later in this book.

Now you could criticize this research because, until recently, most of it was conducted using questionnaires, which were subjective. But with advancement in technology, like brain-scans, FMRIs, and EEGs, psychologists found that there is a very high correlation between the objective measuring like brain-scans and people's evaluation of their well-being through questionnaires.

Ed Diener found that once our basic needs are met (shelter, food, and basic education) income makes little difference in our levels of happiness, except in extreme situations. A homeless person surely might become a lot happier if you pay him or her 2,000 USD a month.

Also when we look around us, we find that our generation is much wealthier than our parents' and grandparents', yet depression and anxiety levels have gone up significantly.

What about your place of residence? Does it make a difference? Well actually it makes very little difference to your happiness.

"If I move to Italy, will I be happier" Yes, for a while, before you go back to your base level.

Science confirms that it makes very little difference to our happiness where we are, where we live, what we earn, if we win the lottery, if we get the promotion, or even if we get the dream job. (One thing that does matter is if you live in a democracy or a dictatorship) And you might say: So why do I work so hard if it doesn't make a difference? Well, it doesn't make a difference, but that doesn't mean that you cannot increase your levels of happiness and well being. And that's the good news: You can increase your basic level of well being.

Another misinterpretation is that a lot of people think that the problem with general levels of happiness and unhappiness is that people have extremely high expectations. So if you lower your expectations, you lower your stress levels, and you will enjoy life more. Wrong again! You will probably be happy for a while but not in the long term.

The problem is not low versus high expectations; the problem is right versus wrong expectations:

It's a wrong expectation that going to a new place, getting a raise, finding your idea of a dream partner is responsible for your happiness. These things will not raise your base level of happiness.

The right expectation is to believe in change from within. Our happiness is mostly dependent on our state of mind, NOT on our status or the state of our bank account. It's about changing our perception, our state of mind, our interpretation of the world, of what's happening to us, of our achievements, and of our failures.

Scientifically speaking, happiness is about what we choose to pursue and what we CHOOSE to focus on.

Accepting our emotions

The last thing I want you to think about after reading this book is that you will experience a constant high and never have any problems anymore. That won't happen. Tal Ben Shahar says that "There are two kinds of people who don't experience painful emotions such as anger, envy, disappointment, sadness, unhappiness or depression: Psychopaths and dead People."

If you experience these emotions, it's a great sign! You are not dead, and you are not a psychopath. However, in our culture, we don't give ourselves what Tal Ben Shahar calls "the permission to be human". We don't give ourselves the freedom to experience these painful emotions as well, although they are an undeniable part of human nature.

As babies and children, we give ourselves the permission to be human. Later, society becomes important for us, and we realize that other people are watching and evaluating us constantly. That's when we stop giving ourselves the permission to be human. The consequences are that our energy levels, our well-being, our happiness, our creativity, and ultimately also our success suffer.

Give yourself the permission to experience painful emotions when you experience it and accept it. That's it. It's human. The worst thing you can do is to suppress an emotion. When we suppress an emotion, the emotion only gets stronger.

It's like when you say "Don't think of a pink elephant." I bet you just visualized a pink elephant, right? The same happens with your emotions. For example, if you are nervous when speaking in front of a crowd and you tell yourself "I'm not nervous, I'm not nervous, I'm not nervous", but when you finally start to speak, you are more nervous than ever. If you are sad and tell yourself "I'm happy, I'm happy, I'm happy", chances are that you end up even more sad and frustrated. You can't trick your emotions, so accept them.

Painful emotions are as much part of the human nature as the law of gravity is part of physical nature or as rain is a part of the climatological nature, and rejecting our nature leads to bad performance. Envy, anger, sadness, depression are part of human nature. There's nothing good or bad about it. They just are. Find a place where you can give yourself the permission to be human. This can be your "me-time" that you use for journaling or being with friends and family.

Giving yourself the permission to be human doesn't mean that you won't have painful emotions anymore. It means that your psychological immune system will get stronger. A stronger immune system doesn't mean that you won't get sick any more (as I always thought), it means that you'll get sick less often and when you do get sick, you'll recover much faster.

The difference between extremely happy and extremely unhappy people is not that unhappy people get sad, upset, anxious or depressed and the happy ones do not. It's how fast you can recover from these painful emotions.

Stop pretending that you are doing fine, when in fact you aren't doing so well. Be honest and say "I'm having a hard time right now. I'm really stressed". Give yourself the permission to be human; there is nothing wrong with you if you experience painful emotions. Happiness doesn't mean that you have to be happy all the time.

Making 'Happiness' the ultimate goal

Another fundamental part to make this whole thing work is to give happiness the highest importance. We have to make it the ultimate end that we pursue. Stop for a moment, take a break from your busy life, and analyze your thoughts. Aren't we spending a lot of time thinking about happiness for ourselves as well as for others?

Aristotle said more than 2,500 years ago: "Happiness is the meaning and purpose of life. The whole aim and end of human existence." William James concluded that "If we were to ask the question 'What is human life's chief concern' one of the answers we should receive would be 'It is happiness'. How to gain, how to keep, and how to recover happiness is, in fact, for most men at all times and the secret motive of all they do."

Last but not the least, the Dalai Lama states "Whether one believes in a religion or not, whether one believes in this religion or that religion. The very purpose of life is happiness. The very motion of our life is toward happiness."

Happiness, or the search for it, transcends cultures, religions, and classes. In my class at the Geneva Business school, there were Christians, Muslims, and Atheists, there were nearly as many nations as students in one room, and we all had one thing in common: wanting to learn how to become happier.

One thing is for sure, and I will show you the scientific proof for it – in case you need it to be convinced – happiness contributes to our life and to our relationships. Happiness helps us to think beyond everyday things, build relationships, and build capacities

In her studies, Barbara Fredrickson found that "Through the experience of positive emotions, people transform themselves to become more creative, knowledgeable, resilient, socially integrated, and healthier individuals."
Yes! Positive emotions do help us overcome negative emotions. While negative emotions narrow and constrict our focus – which is a good thing when you encounter a wild animal and the question is "fight or flight?" – it's not a good thing if it continues beyond the threat.

Positive emotions, on the other hand, broaden, build, and expand our peripheral line of vision.

If for example, my girlfriend or wife leaves me, it's normal that I dwell on it and feel sad for a while. But if after a few months, I still think, "Oh she left me, poor me, how could she do that." I'll spiral down into more sadness and other negative emotions. And if I don't snap out of it, and this feeling starts to persist, then it can turn into depression.

The same goes for positive emotions. Positive emotions can take us out of the downward spiral and create an upward spiral. We can enhance the positive emotions by watching a funny movie, having a good talk with a friend, taking deep breaths, remembering good things from the past, and even by changing our body posture. **It doesn't really take long, but we have to be willing to try it instead of writing it off as nonsense.**

In a study conducted by scientists at the University of Toronto revealed that we even see more of what is around us if we are in a positive mood. The scientists primed people for either positivity or negativity and then let the subjects look at a series of pictures. The results were stunning: People in a negative mood were missing substantial parts of the pictures, while people in a positive mood saw everything.

In another experiment, four-year-old children were asked to put blocks of different shapes together as quickly as they could. One group of the children was asked to think about something that makes them happy. Those kids significantly outperformed the group of children that weren't primed to be positive, they were quicker and had fewer errors.

And here is one study that I often remind my friend Marc, a doctor. In one experiment by Estrada, Isen, and Young, happy doctors came to a diagnosis much faster (twice as fast as a neutral controlled group) and exhibited much more creativity.

So what about other people? How can we talk about or act in our life pursuing OUR happiness? Is that selfish? YES, IT IS! "I want to be happier" That's selfish. But it only becomes bad and immoral in a society where selfishness and immorality have virtually become synonymous.

9

The number one cause of unhappiness, subconsciously or not, is the feeling of guilt associated with pursuing happiness. A lot of times, we are *taught* to feel guilty about feeling good about ourselves. This has to stop! Because it's only when you are happy that you can contribute to other people's happiness and well being. Happiness is the only thing that grows when you give it away, or as they say "You can light thousands of candles with one single candle" This makes happiness a positive addition game. Your happiness is not taking away from other people's happiness, as a matter of fact, most of the time it adds to other people's happiness! Helping others is also helping ourselves, and it feels good to feel good.

If you want to spread happiness, work on your own happiness because then you lead by example and people tend to follow what you do rather than what you say.

2. The Power of Belief

Beliefs create reality

"Your beliefs create your reality." The first time I read this was nearly 30 years ago in the Seth-Material written by Jane Roberts who was channeling Seth. Adventurous and as metaphysical as it gets – I know – nevertheless, over the last 25 years, we've seen a lot of the things that Jane/Seth "wrote" proven by science. And yes, today science can prove that our beliefs really create our reality, and that they are self-fulfilling prophecies.

Remember the study of the most successful people? One of the two characteristics they had was that they believed in themselves. They knew they were going to make it…and the best part is one can *learn* to believe in themselves.

Let's start by looking at beliefs in detail a little later in this chapter. First, here's taking a look at some of the most amazing studies supporting this claim.

Robert Dilts defines beliefs as "judgments and assessments about ourselves, others, and the world around us. A belief is a habitual thought pattern. Once a person believes something is true (whether it's true or not), he or she acts as if it were – collecting facts to prove that belief even if it's false." So each one of us sees the world through the lenses of our own beliefs.

It works like this:
Your beliefs influence your emotions, your emotions influence your actions, and your actions influence your results. So if you want different results, you have to follow the chain backwards. To get a certain result, how do you have to act? And to act in a way to get the result, how do you have to feel? And to feel in a way that makes you act in the way to get the result, what do you have to believe?

Until 1954, it was thought impossible that man could run a mile under four minutes. Doctors and scientists said that it was impossible. There were even scientific papers and studies on the subject. These studies were all shredded on May 6, 1954, when Roger Bannister proved everybody wrong at a race in Oxford when he ran the mile in under four minutes. Just six weeks later, an Australian, John Landy, did the same. In 1955, 37 runners ran the mile under four minutes, and in 1956, over 300 runners. What happened?

It was the power of their MIND. As long as they believed that it was impossible, their subconscious mind prevented them from running faster. Once one man broke the four-minute barrier, the others saw that they could do it too. And they did it.

Our beliefs determine how we perform, how good or bad our relationships are, and a lot of other things. They are the number one predictor of life's successes as well as well-being. So how does it work? How can we raise our beliefs? How can we turn a dream into reality?

"If we treat people as they ought to be, we help them become what they are capable of becoming."

What Goethe already knew hundreds of years ago was proven by the Pygmalion effect. **Our belief in a person's potential brings that potential to life.** When Robert Rosenthal and his team went to an elementary school and did some intelligence tests on the students, they told the teachers that students A, B, and C had extraordinary results and were academic superstars. The teachers could not mention this to the students, nor treat them differently, and to make them understand the seriousness of the project, they were even told that they were being observed.

At the end of the year, the tests were repeated and, to no one's surprise, A, B, and C posted off-the-chart intellectual ability again. Again? Well, the fun thing was that the researchers lied to the teachers the first time around. When tested the first time A, B, and C were absolutely ordinary and randomly picked by the researchers. They concluded that the mere belief of the teacher in the potential of the students brought that potential to life.

Remember this, because the Pygmalion effect can happen anywhere. The expectations you have about your co-workers, your children, your friends, and spouses – whether or not they are ever mentioned – can turn that expectation into reality.

Another amazing experiment was conducted by Ellen Langer in 1979. Langer put a group of 75-year-old men on a one-week retreat in a hotel. These men had to pretend they were 20 years younger. They could bring anything from no later than 1959. There were books, magazines, newspapers, TV shows, news, and pictures from 1959. They dressed like 1959, walked like 1959, even their ID badges had their photos from 1959.

Just before the retreat, they were tested for physical strength, posture, cognition, and short-term memory. So they went on this one-week-retreat, and the results of that experiment were staggering. After the retreat, all of them improved significantly.

Their eyesight improved up to 10%; their hearing and their memory improved significantly; their physical appearance changed; and they became more flexible, stronger, healthier and happier! Both their mental and their physiological age decreased!

All of that just because they entered a powerful positive situation!

Creating a positive situation

You can create a positive situation for yourself. Scientists call it priming.
Priming is when somebody consciously or subconsciously plants a seed, belief, or a picture in your mind and how this, then, influences your behavior.

For example, elderly people who get primed with "old words" like "stick," or "Florida" perform worse on memory tests than people who aren't primed that way. Observers of the experiment even see them walk slower and walk like they were older.

On the other hand, when they are primed with words of achievement like "achievement," "persistence," or "success," they do better in intelligence and memory tests and persist longer in a difficult task

In another experiment, subjects had to describe a typical day in the life of a soccer hooligan, a secretary, and a professor and then did memory and intelligence tests. Guess who performed the worst? The "hooligan" group, while the "professor" group performed the best.

You can use the power of priming and the power of our beliefs by creating a positive environment that brings out the best in you. Here are some examples of how to do that:

- Put up photos of people or places you love
- Put your favorite objects around you (flowers, souvenirs, art, etc.)
- Have your favorite quotes in sight.
- Have your favorite books around you
- Listen to your favorite music
- Watch movies or conferences that inspire you

Believe in yourself

I have great news for you: Self-belief can be learned! It might take some time and some training, like everything else, but you can work on it. Albert Bandera found out that 56% of the success as an athlete is determined by the athlete's levels of hope, and by how much they believe that they are going to succeed. If that works for an athlete, why shouldn't it work for YOU?

Nathaniel Branden, the leading researcher on self-esteem, came to the conclusion that "the level of our self-esteem has profound consequences for every aspect of an existence, how we operate in the workplace, how we deal with people, how high we are likely to rise, how much we are likely to achieve, with whom do we end up falling in love, how we interact with our spouse, children and friends, and what level of personal happiness we attain."

Changing your performance by changing your beliefs

You have a choice. You can see pain, negativity, stress or you can look at things with the lens of optimism, gratitude, hope, resilience, and purpose. You might not be able to change reality, but you can and should use your brain to change how you process the world around you, and that will change how you react to what happens to you. It's time that you use the power of your beliefs to change your reality.

Do you need more proof for the power of your beliefs? Here we go:
Take for example, the **Placebo Effect**. It works like this: You have a headache, you see a doctor, the doctor prescribes you a pill, you take the pill, 30 minutes later, the headache is gone. No surprises, until now. But what if the doctor gave you a sugar water pill (placebo) instead of an Aspirin. What got rid of your headache? Right, your belief that the pill would cure you. As a matter of fact, a placebo is 55-60% as effective as medicine.

Herbert Benson took it a little further. He treated pregnant women who were nauseous with a placebo and surprise, surprise, they felt better after taking the pill. They cured themselves with their belief alone. But Herbert didn't stop there. The next time around he gave them a small dose of ipecac, a pill that induces vomiting. So the pregnant women should feel even more nauseous as they already felt. But they didn't know that they were taking an ipecac, so they got better!

This doesn't mean that drugs don't have any effect, but it shows the enormous power of the mind, and we shouldn't discard it.

15

The most incredible experiment though was mentioned in the New York Times and was done by some Japanese researchers – and I have no idea how they got permission for this. The researchers rubbed the arms of thirteen unknowing students with a harmless plant and told them that it was poison ivy. All 13 showed symptoms (a mean rash). In the next round, they rubbed their arms with real poison ivy but told them it was a harmless plant, and only two students showed symptoms. Based on these incredible results, the researchers came to the conclusion that our brain is organized to act on what we expect what will happen next.

So yes, our beliefs turn into fulfilling prophecies. They can actually change the concrete results of our efforts and our work. That's why "self-concept is destiny."

A.J Crum and E. Langer show this best in an experiment they did with the cleaning staff of different hotels. They formed two groups. Group one was told to think of their work as exercise, while group 2 was told nothing. After only six weeks, the members of group 1 had actually lost weight and their cholesterol levels dropped. The only difference between the two groups was in how their brains perceived the work they were doing!

We learn from these studies that your beliefs about our daily activities define our reality more than the activities themselves. Amazing, isn't it? How much more productive and efficient could you be if you changed the way you see the hours in your work day?

Be careful! If you believe that time with your family or free time is not productive, you will make it, in fact, a waste of time. Train yourself to adopt better beliefs about your time, like for example, looking at it as a chance to learn new things, a time to recharge your batteries, or to connect with others. If you manage it, you will return stronger and more relaxed than ever before.

And there is even more! Applying the placebo and the Pygmalion effect, it's safe to say that the more you believe in your ability to succeed, the more likely you are to do so. It's even more important that you believe that you can improve them, that you can enhance your basic qualities through training and effort, and therefore, maximize your potential. This is what psychologists call a "growth mindset."

On the other hand, you have the "fixed mindset." People with a fixed mindset think that their capabilities are already set and that they can't change them. People who think like this usually miss opportunities for improvement and underperform consistently.

So remember: If you believe you'll do well, you'll probably do well. I'd love to make it more complicated, but it really is that easy. The hard part is the daily work and training you have to do to reach that level of self-belief.

Our reality really depends on how we view it. Shawn Achor mentions in his book "The Happiness Advantage" that positive psychologists found out that external circumstances predict only 10% of our happiness! 10%!

That means that if I knew everything about you. Where you live, in which country, in a house or an apartment, where you work, your salary, the car you drive, etc. I could still only predict 10% of your happiness.

Once again: The way you perceive these external circumstances is much more important for your happiness than the circumstances themselves. By changing the way, you perceive your circumstances, your work, and yourself, you can dramatically improve our results.

Being an optimist helps

Even if you think that you are born an optimist or pessimist, being an optimist or a pessimist ultimately comes down to one thing: How do you interpret events?

Do you interpret an event as permanent (never) or as temporary (one step closer)?

Do you see failure as a catastrophe and give up or do you see it as an opportunity for success?

In the last two years, I failed more than in the total 41 years of my life. Really, I had at least one failure a week for the last two years. It's also no coincidence that this was the two best and most successful years of my life. Because with a lot of failures automatically comes more success. It's a numbers game. If I have to be rejected 15 times to get a well-paid speaking gig, I take this equation any time.

Back to interpretations, I'm sure you have heard the story about Thomas Edison who considered his 10,000 failed attempts to create the light bulb not as failure, but as showing 10,000 ways of what doesn't work.

When Dean Simonton studied the most successful scientists and artists through history, he found out that they were also the ones who failed the most.

Many remember Babe Ruth as one of the greatest baseball players of all times and for his home run records, but few people know that the seasons where he had the most home runs, were also the seasons when he had the most strikeouts. He said it himself: "Every strike brings me closer to the next home run."

If you can internalize that way of interpreting failure, nothing can stop you. Twenty phone calls to make one sale. I take it. Fifteen rejections for one speaking gig. I take it. Thirty job interviews to score my dream job. I take it. There is no other way to learn. There is no other way to succeed. That's how you learn to walk, that's how you learn to eat. Learn to fail or fail to learn. Fail often. Fail fast.

Learning to interpret events optimistically leads to much higher success. It also strengthens our biological and psychological immune system. And last, but not the least...Optimists live longer, which doesn't mean that all pessimists die young because there are more things to factor in.

It also doesn't mean that all optimists live long. If you smoke 40 cigarettes a day, being an optimist might not help a lot.

And there is another crucial thing to be careful about: **False optimism, sooner or later, leads to disillusion, anger, and hopelessness.** We need to train to become "realistic optimists." Positive thinking alone is not enough. You also have to add optimism, passion, and hard work to the success formula.

Why did nobody ever teach us this? It might be because the countless studies about the influence of happiness in our success are only surfacing now. As I said in the beginning, twenty years ago, you could either believe it or disregard it. Now you have science to back it up, which is hard to deny.

Another reason is that our parents are often concerned about us, about our happiness, and about our self-esteem. They don't want us to be disappointed. They think that too high expectations will lead to disappointment, but that is totally wrong. False expectations lead to disappointment.

In this case, the false expectation is that events can make us happy or unhappy. That's wrong. **Science found out that there are ups and downs around a base level of well being. These ups and downs in life are inevitable, how you deal with them is your choice.** The good news is that you can take more risks. If you cope instead of avoiding, if you confront things, if you take risks, if you deal with things, if you go out and try, your base level of happiness increases and that's what it's all about.

The self-perception theory states that we derive conclusions about ourselves the same way we derive conclusions about others: By looking at behavior. So if we behave like people with self-esteem, our self-esteem rises. We think of ourselves "I must be a self-confident person" and then it becomes a self-fulfilling prophecy, and we become more self-confident.

We'll talk about failure in another chapter a little later, but let me just mention: The pain that comes with failure is far lesser than the pain that we *think* comes with it. Once we realize this, we become more confident telling ourselves "I can deal with this. I can handle it. I'm actually more resilient than I thought I was". Your self-esteem increases, your happiness increases, and finally, success comes. There is no other way to succeed.

The three keys to success

First of all, you HAVE to take ACTION. There is no way around it. If you find a way to succeed without taking action and hard work, please let me know. I've worked 40 to 60 hours per week in the last three years, including weekends. I think hard work is the only way to succeed, but I'm open to your feedback. Hard work and coping inevitably lead to success.

Taking actions is important. If you only talk about what you will be doing but don't take actions, you will not accomplish anything. It can actually even harm you. Even positive self-talk and positive affirmations can harm. If you only talk, but then avoid challenges, or constantly avoid difficult experiences and don't give yourself the permission to fail, you end up creating a downward spiral regarding your self-esteem, which affects your success and well being. Only talking and not doing sends a message to yourself that says "my word isn't worth anything, I'm not worth anything" and this will definitely affect your self-esteem. So take actions instead of just talking.

The second key is visualizing your success. The three components of success are optimism, believing in yourself, and loving what you do.

Stephen Kosselyn found out that whether you look at your hand or whether you imagine it, the same neurons are firing. This means that for your brain there is no difference! That's incredible and was even promoted by self-help gurus for a long time. Now it's scientifically proven, and YES I'll say it one more time: For our brain, there is no difference between imagination and the real thing.

Athletes use visualization, sales people use it too, and so can you. If you are imagining success, you are fooling your mind into believing that it's the real thing. For me personally, I visualize only the outcome; the destination I desire, while I leave the rest to destiny, God, the universe, life or whatever you want to call it. There is some fascinating science about this subject though.

Shelley Taylor from UCLA did the following research:
She took two random groups. Group 1 was imagining themselves over and over again getting an A. Group 2 was imagining themselves getting an A, but also seeing themselves work and persist in the library, prepare for the exam, and then get an A. In this experiment, the second group was much more successful!

Last, but not the least, remember that thoughts drive emotions. If you want to change the emotion, you have to change your thoughts

EVENT —> EVALUATION (Thought) —> EMOTION —> ACTION

A lot of times, in our evaluation of a situation, we distort reality and have irrational thoughts. There are three traps of irrational thoughts, which we should closely look at when they surface.

1. **Magnifying** (overgeneralizing)– For example, you fail one exam, and because of that, you think that you are stupid. Or one person says no to you, and that makes you think that nobody wants you, or your product. You had one bad experience on a Tuesday afternoon, and you think you had a terrible week.

2. **Minimizing** (tunnel vision)– This happens when you focus on the one person that is asleep in your presentation and not at the 200 that are highly interested. You concentrate on one critical comment and not

on the ten people that praised you. If you catch yourself with these irrational thoughts, look at the bigger picture and zoom out.

3. **Making up** (fabricating)– This unfortunately often happens to abused people. They think it's their fault because they have not been behaving appropriately. Which it is of course NOT true! Another example would be failing an exam and blaming your girlfriend/boyfriend for that, which is utter nonsense.

The following questions can help you deal with irrational thoughts:

- Is my conclusion tied to reality?
- Is it rational?
- Am I ignoring something important?
- What important evidence do I still have to take into consideration?
- What am I magnifying?
- What am I minimizing?
- Am I ignoring something that's going well?
- Am I ignoring something that's not going very well?
- What is the big picture?

As always, it comes down to choice. Whatever we do with our beliefs, we can create an upward or a downward spiral!

3. The Power of Focus

As I already mentioned, one of the most decisive influences of your daily happiness is your focus. You can retrain your brain to see more of the good things in life. Doing this, will help you see more opportunities, more possibilities, feel more energetic, and lastly, succeed at higher levels.

Where is your focus? In the past or the present? On problems or solutions? Do you celebrate your successes or do you take them for granted? How do you see failure? Is it a disaster, an opportunity to grow, or a learning experience? Everything depends on where you put your attention.

Does this sound familiar to you? You are thinking about buying a new car, and suddenly the car you're considering to buy is everywhere? You are pregnant, and suddenly there are pregnant women everywhere. Or you have a cast, and suddenly everyone seems to have a cast? When we look for something, we see it everywhere. Or you hear a song once, and suddenly every radio station starts playing it. You buy new clothes – suddenly everybody seems to be wearing something similar. This is how focus works. Once your focus is on something, you start to see it everywhere. This is great when you focus on the positive, on opportunities, on things that make you happy; and not so great when you focus on worries, problems, and sadness.

Two people can view the same situation and actually see different things depending on what they are expecting to see. They don't just come away with different interpretations of the event – they have actually seen different things in their visual field.

Ed Diener describes the power of focus in the following way
"How we perceive the world is much more important to happiness than objective circumstances. It's not the external that matters; it's the internal. It depends on our state of mind – on what we CHOOSE to focus on."

In the end, how we experience our life is a matter of interpretation, a matter of choice, and it's up to us what we choose.

When we complain about life and how things are horrible and awful for us, we often do not realize that we are causing this. We imagine the worst, and then the Pygmalion effect kicks in and our beliefs become self-fulfilling prophecies, or we focus on what's not working and then we see more and more of what is not working. It seems like we are attracting it.

WE ACTUALLY CREATE OUR REALITY.

The questions you ask determine your reality, they change the way you perceive reality. You transform your reality by changing your focus on what's working, and by asking new questions. These new questions will create a new reality for you.

Tal Ben-Shahar distinguishes the following type of people in his classes at Harvard.

On one hand, there is the "Benefit Finder," whose focus is always on what works, always looking on the bright side of life, making lemonade out of lemons, finding the miracle in the common, and respecting reality. The benefit finder knows that sometimes we are not responsible for things that happen, but we are responsible for how we deal with what happens to us. Simply said: Shit happens, but it's up to us what we do with the experience.

The "Fault Finder" on the other hand always focuses on what doesn't work, on things that are not going well, on problems. "Fault Finders" are constant complainers who find faults even in the best of situations. This is very dangerous because it can lead to resignation. They do not recognize that they create that reality. They think that the terrible reality is out there and that they are victims of their circumstances. So they feel miserable most of the time. No matter what job they find, they always have a horrible boss. No matter what partners they have, they are always awful and inconsiderate. No matter what restaurant they go to, the service is always terrible. And when the service is excellent, the food is terrible. There is always something. They accept that reality as given and their existence becomes a very painful self-fulfilling prophecy.

The good news is: We can learn to become "Benefit Finders" by training our brains to focus on the positive, by learning to interpret things optimistically. As Tal Ben Shahar always says: "Things don't happen for the best, but some people are able to make the best of things that happen." Yes, there are some people who accept the situation and then are able to make the best of it. Become one of such people. A "Benefit Finder" always knows: "This too shall pass," "It's going to be alright again," and "Been there done that." The "Benefit Finder" accepts reality as it is, makes the best of it, and therefore reaps the benefits of this behavior like feeling better, being happier in the long term, experiencing more positive moods, and being less likely to feel anxious.

Health benefits

Being a "Benefit Finder" is also healthier for you. Glen Affleck was studying people who had a heart attack. Some of the patients interpreted their health problems as a catastrophe, or at the end of the world, while the "Benefit Finders" saw it as a wake-up call, as a sign to take better care of themselves, and revise their values. The second group was more likely to survive and less likely to have a second heart attack.

Another study on AIDS patients revealed that those who found benefits in their situation, like for example appreciating things more, focusing on the things that really matter, or getting closer to certain people, were more likely to survive.

The most famous study on health benefits of optimism is the so-called "Nun Study" which showed that joy prolongs our life.

The study started in 1932 when 178 nuns, about the age of 22, were tested on numerous accounts. They had to write biographical sketches of themselves, and scientists looked at various factors. There was only one predictor for longevity: Positive feelings.

The researchers looked at the writings and categorized them into four categories. Most positive, least positive, and two categories in between.

After 85 years, 90% of the most-positive category and only 34% of the least-positive category were alive. After 90 years, 54% of the most-positive category and only 11% of the least-positive category were alive. Careful now, that doesn't mean that there weren't some "Fault Finders" who lived long, nor were there some "Benefit Finders" that died earlier. But on an average, "Benefit Finders" or optimists live longer.

Why aren't we all optimists?

We have a lot of proof that optimism makes you happier and healthier so we might ask ourselves "If optimism has such great benefits why isn't everyone optimistic?" Why does nobody teach us how to become more optimistic? Why does nobody tell us about these benefits in the first place? Why are optimists considered detached?

One reason for this is the media. We mostly see hatred, bloodshed, unhappiness, terrorism, corruption, and fraud. How can you be positive in a world like this? What most of us forget is that the media doesn't just report reality as it is. It's biased towards the negative. The news actually turns us into pessimists by magnifying the negative. We are shown terror when billions of people want to live in peace. We are shown fraud when there are billions of honest transactions going on every day. We are shown that one parent who abuses their child when there are millions of parents loving their children beyond measure.

The problem with that is that if our focus is on the negative all the time, if we hear and see this all the time, we'll end up seeing more of it. And then we start to believe that we have to commit fraud to become a CEO, or to be corrupt if we want to be politicians. Why? Because the millions of people who are succeeding honestly are not reported on.

I don't want you to ignore the negative, but focus on the positive. And yes, I turned off the box a long, long time ago. Try it. It's great. And don't worry, you won't become ignorant or detached from reality when you stop watching TV. It's actually the "Fault Finder" who is detached because there is much more good in the world than bad. Focus on the positive. It's important, not just because it's healthier, but because FOCUS CREATES REALITY.

The same goes for your inner dialogue. For many people it's a constant negative chatter in our mind, why is it negative and not positive? You know the typical "Why didn't I do this, why didn't I do that," "What if this goes wrong," "What if they don't like me." We are constantly dress-rehearsing drama in our life. Why? Because everything around us focuses on the negative. No worries, it can be fixed. You fix it by rewiring your brain to see more of the positive around you and the best exercise to do for this is practicing gratitude. If you are grateful for the things you have, more things to be grateful for will come into your life.

And yes, there is always something to be grateful for. Believe me. Even cancer patients and AIDS patients found reasons to be grateful for. When terminally-ill patients were interviewed, they said things like "For the first time in my life I feel that I'm alive" or "For the first time in my life I appreciate…

The Power of Gratitude

The sad thing is that a lot of times things have to get really bad before we appreciate what we have. It doesn't have to be that way if we learn the attitude of gratitude as a way of life. If I would have to name the single-most important ingredient of my success or why my life is so much better, and I, so much happier, than even some a short while ago, it would be because of gratitude.

A lot of times we just don't express gratitude enough. But that can be practiced. It means we should express gratitude over and over again until it becomes a habit.

In a study conducted by Robert Emmons and Michael McCullough from UC Davis, people who wrote down five things for which they were grateful every night before going to bed, were more optimistic, happier, healthier, more generous, benevolent, and much more likely to achieve their goals than the three other groups who didn't write down anything, wrote down 5 hassles, or wrote down 5 things they are better at than others.

You cultivate gratitude by doing it all the time. Write down the big things and the little things. When I started writing three to five things that I was grateful for every night on November 11, 2013, it was the little things that came to my mind:

- I'm grateful that I'm alive
- I'm grateful for my family
- I'm grateful for my friends
- I'm grateful for the cup of coffee I had on the beach
- I'm grateful for working hard
- I'm grateful for that good lunch that I had with a friend
- I'm grateful for that good presentation I attended.
- I'm grateful for a sunny day.

It's important that you FEEL the gratitude and that not do it mechanically. Feel the gratitude with your whole body. Visualize and make it as real as you can.

Tal Ben Shahar notes that it's better to do it once a week MINDFULLY than to do it every day automatically without caring for it. The important thing is the intensity of the emotion.

Apart from doing the three things daily I also have a gratitude list where I write down everything I'm grateful for in my life. This should be a long list. For me, it includes places I've visited, people I've met, vacations I took, and other such things. If you read this list once a day and add to it frequently, the gratitude effect gets bigger. Try it, it can make a lot of difference. Imagine how your days will start if you read your gratitude list first thing in the morning! And as they say, the start of the day determines how the rest of the day goes.

This exercise is the bomb. After a while, you start noticing things. It's so powerful because you are co-creating your reality with it focusing on all the things you can be grateful for in your life.

If you practice gratitude throughout a few weeks, you'll be happier, more optimistic, more socially connected; you'll sleep better and get fewer headaches; you'll have more energy, more emotional intelligence; and you'll be more forgiving, less likely to be depressed, anxious, or lonely.

In my class at the Geneva Business School, one of the homework assignments was writing down three things the students were grateful for every day. I saw exactly the benefits mentioned above when reading their assignments over the week.

You might say "Of course, these people are only grateful because they are happier", but it's the other way round: Gratitude has been proven to be a significant cause of positive outcomes.

I know it can be difficult to be grateful when you are in a bad place, and life is not going so well, but believe me, there is always something to be grateful for. The most essential thing: You are breathing, you are alive, and there is somebody who cares for you. Start there, you'd be surprised by how long the list can run.

Focus on the positive

The more you focus on happiness, gratitude, optimism, the more you pick up on all the positive things around you and the better you will feel.

But there is more to it. The more your brain picks up on the positive, the more you'll expect this trend to continue, which results in you being more optimistic. You are creating a self-fulfilling prophecy and an upward spiral.

Optimism is also one of the most powerful predictors of work performance:
Optimists set more goals and put more efforts into attaining these goals. They stay more committed in the face of difficulties and overcome obstacles more easily. They cope better with high-stress situations, and expecting positive outcomes makes them more possible to bounce back.

Are some people just lucky?

Richard Wiseman asks the question of questions "Why do some of us seem to be constantly lucky while others can't get a break?"

He adds: **"In science, there is no such thing as luck. The only difference is whether or not people think they are lucky or not. Whether they expect good things or bad things to happen to them."**

And he did a study on it: Subjects were to read through a newspaper and count how many photos are in it. Those who claimed to be lucky took mere seconds, while the unlucky ones took an average of two minutes. Why? Because on the second page of the newspaper, a very large message said "Stop counting. There are 43 photos in this newspaper".

The answer was plain as day, but people who considered themselves as unlucky were far more likely to miss it while the lucky people tended to see it.

But Wiseman didn't stop there. Half way through the newspaper there was another message that said: "Stop counting and help tell the experimenter you have seen this, and you win $150 USD". And once again the people who claimed to be unlucky in life looked right past this opportunity. Stuck in the negative focus, they were unable of seeing what was clear to others and their performance (and wallets) suffered because of it.

Another study found out that 69% of high school and college students' career decisions depend on chance encounters.

As we learned from the study explained above capitalizing or not on these meetings is purely a matter of focus! When we are stuck in negativity, our brain is literally incapable of seeing these opportunities. If we are positive, our brain stays open to seeing these opportunities and to seizing them.

The amazing thing is that if we expect a favorable outcome, our brain is actually programmed to notice the outcome when it actually arises

Train your brain on focusing on the positive

You can train your brain to focus on the positive, and as a result of that, see more opportunities with two very easy exercises:

1. Make a daily list of all the good things that have happened to you in your job, career, and life
2. At night, remember three good things that happened to you that day and relive them in your mind

Don't get fooled by the simplicity of these exercises. They are very powerful. I hold them primarily responsible for my success, for seeing opportunities everywhere now.

If you do this for just FIVE MINUTES a day, you are training your brain to become better at noticing and focusing on possibilities of personal and professional growth and also on seizing them and acting on them.

At the same time, there is a great side effect: your brain can only concentrate on so much at once, so it will push out those little things that annoy you and the nagging negative voices at the back of your mind.

Doing this exercise for just one week will make you happier and less depressed, and you'll see a marked difference after one, three and six months. Even after stopping the exercise you'll remain significantly happier, and show higher levels of optimism. I highly recommend you to keep on doing this exercise as it will do miracles for you. You'll get better and better in scanning the world for good things and writing them down, and you'll see more and more opportunities – without even trying – wherever you look.

The things you write down don't need to be complicated or profound, only specific. A lot of times, it's the simple things like a child's smile, delicious food, acknowledgment at work, a moment of connection with Nature etc.

Make this a habit and ritualize it. Do it at the same time each day. Keep what you need for doing this exercise easily available and convenient. For example, a journal on your night stand. It's also enjoyable to do the exercise with children and spouses.

Will you be blind to the real problems if you only focus on the good?
This is a question that comes up often. It's something you have to find out for yourself. My suggestion is to let the really big problems into your field of vision, but stick to keeping your focus largely on the positive. I can't deny that there are times when it's good to be a pessimist. Pessimism can, for example, stop us from making a foolish investment, or a bad career move, or from gambling with our health. That's why we have to develop a realistic, healthy, and reasonable sense of optimism, but above all, always give priority to the good.

4. The Power of Choice

This is your incredible power. Free will and the power of choice. Even if you can't always control the things that happen to you, you can always control how they will affect you and how you react to them.

Choose your thoughts

First of all, it is about choosing the right thoughts. James Allen said, "You are today where your thoughts have brought you; you will be tomorrow where your thoughts take you." Your thoughts create your reality. You can actually improve your life by improving your thoughts. How is that done? Just like James Allen said: Observe your thoughts now and then. By controlling your thoughts, you ultimately control your life and destiny.

I know it sounds cheesy and easier than it is, but I'll still say it: Think positive! A person who thinks positively is not a dreamer, who thinks there are no problems in life. Instead, he or she recognizes that problems are opportunities to grow, and knows that they only have the meaning that they are given. Positive thinking is to see reality as it is, accept it, and make the best of it.

Train your mind to concentrate only on positive, creative, and inspiring thoughts. Remember what the power of focus does. If you train your mind like this for a while, you will see that the circumstances of your life change too.

You are the creator of your thoughts, but you are not your thoughts. Your thoughts are energy, and the energy follows the thought. Thoughts create emotions, which create behavior, which creates actions, and those actions have consequences in your daily life. Practice a thought often enough so that it becomes a belief, and your behavior and actions will follow its lead.

THOUGHT ->   EMOTION   ->   BEHAVIOR   ->   ACTION

For example, if you constantly worry about not having enough money, you'll create behaviors based on fear. You'll play smaller. You'll try to hang on to the money you have versus playing to win.

Your thoughts depend on your beliefs about life. If you don't like what you are receiving then have a look at what you are sending! Remember that everything, or at least the vast majority of things, that you have in your life has been created by your thoughts, expectations, and beliefs. So analyze them, if you change your beliefs, you will get new results. Of course, there are horrible things in life that you haven't created, like for example being abused, or being exploited, or a close one dying. BUT you can still CHOOSE how these horrible things affect you. I guarantee you will find people, who went through the same, and still thrived. In fact, came out stronger. Take those people as role models.

Choose your emotions

Emotion is energy in motion, a physical reaction to a thought.
Who is responsible for how you feel? YOU! Your emotions come from your thoughts, and you are in control of your thoughts. If you can control your thoughts, you are also capable of controlling your emotions.

Don't be scared by your emotions. They are a part of you, but they are not YOU. Accept them. They are part of human nature, and every emotion has its function. Fear protects you. Anger allows you to defend yourself, put limits on things, and show others what bothers you. Sadness allows you to mourn and identify a lack.

Be connected to your emotions, know how to express them, and do not neglect them.

Don't fool yourself and say "I'm happy" if you're not. Instead, analyze where the emotion comes from. Don't identify yourself with the feeling. I repeat, you are not your emotions!

34

Become an observer and watch where your emotions lead you.
Observe them and watch them pass by like the clouds on a blue sky.
Accept them like you accept rainy days. When you look out of the window, and it rains you don't think that it will rain all the time now, do you? You accept the rain as part of the Nature's plan, that doesn't mean that it will rain all the time.

You can do the same thing with anger, sadness, fear, etc. Just because they show up at one moment in time doesn't mean that they will be there forever. Remember, emotions are neither bad nor good. They just are. Sometimes, it helps to write about them to get them out of your system. Write the angry letter to a person that hurt you. Just writing will help you blow off some steam. I recommend you not to send it though.

For example, I write my angry e-mails and then let them rest for a day. If on the next day I read it and I still resonate with it, then only I send it...In 99% of the cases, it goes to the trash.

Emotions are messengers that we can feel in our body. Listen to them! If you are hooked to an emotion, you are hooked to the past, and you are losing the present. Ask yourself what it is that you really need and then stop searching in the outside and start searching inside of you.

The skill to perceive, use, understand, and manage emotions is also called "managing our emotions." So how does that work? And with whom?

You can use this skill on yourself or others. It works the following way:
1) Perceive and express emotions (Permit yourself to feel it).
2) Facilitation of feelings (How can I feel a different emotion).
3) Understanding (Why is this emotion coming up).
4) Emotional adjustment (Now I know why that emotion surfaced).
The first step is to identify your emotions and explore them, which means to permit their expression and then analyze the problems that provoked them. Connect and talk to the emotion, breathe, relax, and relive the situation.

Once again, everything is a question of attitude (acceptance or refusal). YOU CHOOSE!

Advantages of managing of emotions:

- You recover better and faster from problems and setbacks.
- You achieve better, and make consistent professional performance.
- You can prevent build up of those tensions that destroy your relationships.
- You govern your impulses and conflicting emotions.
- You stay balanced and calm, even in critical moments.

Choose to take responsibility for your life

Sigmund Freud said, "Most people do not really want freedom because freedom involves responsibility, and most people are frightened of responsibility." I have bad news for you my friend: NO ONE IS COMING TO SAVE YOU! No guru, no prince, no millionaire, not even the lottery.

There is only one person that's responsible for the happiness in your life, and that is YOU! Not your boss, not your spouse, not your parents, not your friends, not your clients, not the economy, not the government. YOU!

Now that the elephant is out of the room, let's get to the good news:
The day we stop blaming others for everything that happens in our life and take full responsibility for our life and everything that happens to you, everything changes. Taking responsibility for your life is taking charge of your life and becoming the protagonist of it.

You go from being a victim of the circumstances to creating your own circumstances, or at least, you get the power to decide how you are going to act in the face of circumstances that life presents to you.

36

More good news:

It doesn't matter what happens to you in your life; it matters what attitude you adopt. And the attitude you adopt is your choice. If you are in a bad situation right now, I bet that there are hundreds or thousands of people in this world that have been in this situation and overcame it. That means that you can do it, too.

If you blame your life situation on others, what has to happen to make your life better? All of the others have to change! And that my friend – I assure you – is not going to happen.

On the other hand, if you are the protagonist, YOU have the power to change the things that you don't like in your life! And a lot of times, if you change, everything around you starts changing too.

Remember that it's you who is in control of your thoughts, actions, and feelings. You are in control of your words, the series you watch on TV, and the people you spend your time with.

Stop reacting to others and start responding. Reaction is automatic. Responding is consciously choosing your response. If you don't like your results, change your input, your thoughts, emotions, and expectations.

Let's look a little closer at the Victim and Protagonist archetypes:

The victim thinks that he or she depends on external factors; they feel powerless because the belief is that life happens to them and they can't change anything. Their focus is mostly outside of them and they are focused on excuses like crisis, age, "not a good time," etc.

The victim concentrates on problems, and most of the time, those are everybody else's fault. Because the victim is always right. Life is not fair to them, and everything is just a matter of luck, which you can't influence.

Every bad thing in a victim's life is the fault of others; the victim only reacts; is always innocent; and is constantly blaming others for his or her life situation.

The victim uses the past as justification for putting his or her hope always on a future that will miraculously bring solutions to problems or a change in others who are causing the troubles.

On the other hand, you have the protagonist, the person taking full responsibility for his or her life. Protagonists don't wait for change to come; they initiate it. People of this group are aware that life happens, but they are still free to choose their behavior in any given circumstances. Their focus is always inside of them. They see themselves with options and the power of choice and know that success only depends on them. For example, if they are unhappy at work, instead of complaining, they start looking for alternatives. They are always focused on solutions; they fully understand that they have to act where they have control, and accept situations where they don't have control. Protagonists don't believe in luck, they believe in work. They make their own luck focusing on opportunities, creating them if necessary, and always hold themselves accountable.

Protagonists know that they are responsible for their life, and choose the adequate behavior; they use the past as a valuable experience from which to learn; live in the present where they see constant opportunities for change; and then decide and go after the future goals.

If you are not part of the problem, you also can't be part of the solution. If the problem is caused by the outside that you have no influence on, then the solution is also on the outside that you have no influence on. In that case, you are helpless. You have to hope that the solution magically comes through an outside force. For example, if you go late to work because of "traffic," what has to happen so that you can get to work on time? Traffic has to disappear magically. Because as long as there is traffic, you will always be late. If you act like a protagonist, your being on time doesn't depend on the traffic. It depends on you leaving home early.

Another example: It rains a lot, and you get soaked. If you ask a victim "Why are you soaked?" they will tell you, "Because it rained." A protagonist's answer would be "Because I didn't take my umbrella." So once again, even if you don't have control over the stimuli that the environment sends to you continuously, you have the liberty to choose your behavior in facing the situation. This leads us to the most important question: "Who will you choose to be – by your actions – when life presents you with these circumstances?"

More choices...

Your life is the result of the decisions you take. How do you feel about that? Is this true for you? It's important that from now on, you are aware of the power you have over your life by making decisions!

Every decision, every choice has an important influence on your life. In fact, your life is a direct result of the choices and decisions you've made in the past, and every choice carries a consequence.

The most important thing is to make decisions. Whether the decision is right or wrong is secondary. You will soon receive feedback that will help you to progress. Once you have made a decision, go with it and face the consequences. If it was wrong, learn from it and forgive yourself knowing that at that point in time and with the knowledge you had, it was the best and the right decision to take.

Victor Frankl was a Jewish psychologist imprisoned in Germany's concentration camps during the Second World War. He lost his entire family, except for his sister. Under these terrible circumstances, he became aware of what he named "the ultimate human freedom", which not even the Nazi prison wards could take away from him; they could control his external circumstances, but in the last instance it was he who CHOSE HOW these circumstances were going to affect him!

He found that between STIMULUS and RESPONSE, there was a small space in time in which he had the freedom to CHOOSE his RESPONSE!

This means that even if you may not be able to control the circumstances that life presents to you, you can always choose your

39

response to those circumstances, and by doing so, have a huge impact on your life.

In other words: What hurts us is not what happens to us, but our response to what happens to us.

The most important thing is HOW we RESPOND to what happens to us in our lives. And that my friend is a CHOICE!

Do you want to be healthier? Make better choices about food and exercise.

Do you want to be more successful? Make better decisions about who you surround yourself with, what you read, and what you watch. There are no excuses!

CHOOSING to do things even has health benefits!

The following experiment was conducted at an old age home:
Subjects were divided into two groups. Group 1 got everything. Group 2 had to do everything themselves. They had to water their plants, and they had to tell the employees if they needed something, which they then had to get themselves. They did their own thing independently.

After 18 months, the members of Group 2 were less likely to be depressed. They were healthier, happier, had more energy and…they were 50% more likely to be alive.

The only difference between the groups was CHOICE!

Do you have to or do you choose to?

Are there many things in your life that you "should," but never do? Should you exercise more, go to the gym more, stop smoking, eat healthier, and spend more time with your family? How many of those "shoulds" do you have in your life? They don't help you to get anywhere; they only give you a bad conscience and open the gates to self-torture: "Why am I not going to the gym? I'm so bad! I will never lose weight", "I'm not good enough."

Make a list of all the "shoulds" that drain your energy and then forget it!

If you have had a goal since last year and didn't do anything about it, then you are better off forgetting about it. If your goal is going to the gym and you didn't go for a year, let it go. With the goal, you also let go of the bad conscience and the self-punishment for not accomplishing it. Throw out all your "shoulds" and set some new goals!

Try substituting "I should" and "I have to" with "I choose to," "I decide to," "I will" and "I prefer to" for a while and see how it makes you feel. Say things like "I choose to exercise more," "I will eat healthier," "I will read more." It's important that you enjoy your activities – if not, don't do them.

So get out a piece of paper now and make a list of your "shoulds." Once you're done, either let go of them or rephrase them to "I choose to" or "I decide to."

Stop these toxic habits

Stop making excuses. You don't have to agree with a lot of things with the "Wolf of Wall Street" Jordan Belfort, but with one thing he was surely spot on: "The only thing standing between you and your goal is the bullshit story you keep telling yourself as to why you can't achieve it." And you, my friend, are choosing what you are telling yourself. It might be a subconscious choice at first, but it's still a choice.

It's natural that once you start getting out of your comfort zone, excuses start popping up. It happens to all of us at some point in life. Fear and doubts make you come up with the "best" excuses: "It's not the right moment", "I'm too young", "I'm too old", "It's impossible", "I can't", and my favourite one, "I have no money". Guess what people with money say: "I have no time."

You can choose not to listen to these excuses. You can choose to move ahead in spite of fear and excuses. You can choose to feel uncomfortable and take actions or to make up an excuse. Try it. It's fun!

The second toxic habit is the habit of complaining. I share Lou Holtz' opinion: "Never tell your problems to anyone... 20% don't care and the other 80% are glad you have them." Complaining posions your attempts of becoming happier. It's an absolutely useless behavior that encourages self-pity and doesn't accomplish anything. It's not attractive at all. It's the mentality of a victim.

I was also a huge complainer till I learned the concept of the victim and the protagonist. I decided to give it a try. Instead of complaining about not having time, I got up an hour earlier. Instead of complaining about my weight, I started living a healthier lifestyle and eating cleaner. Instead of blaming my parents, my teachers, my boss, society, the government, or the economy, I took responsibility for my life. I worked hard in the last three years during the toughest crisis Spain saw in decades, and I prospered.

Take responsibility. It's really nobody's fault that you smoke so much, that you eat unhealthy food, or that you give up on your dreams, but your own. It's you who pushes the snooze button instead of getting up half an hour earlier and who chooses fear over risk. Don't blame others for not living a satisfying life. Don't even blame yourself. Blaming is useless too. Just use that energy and get to work or reflect on what you really, really want.

You own your life! You can do anything you want with it. The sooner you get this, the sooner you can move on in the direction of your dreams. Just remember where to focus!

Complaining about your present circumstances will put your focus on them and attract more of what you don't like. You have to get out of this vicious circle and concentrate on what you want instead
This will make you will feel like you are in control of your life, and that will do miracles for you.

Take control

The belief that we have control, that our behavior matters, that we are the masters of our own destiny at home and work is one of the biggest drivers of well-being and success. And the best thing is, it doesn't even matter how much control we really have. It's more about how much control we think we have.

Shawn Achor shows us in his book "The Happiness Advantage" that students who feel in control have higher levels of happiness, higher grades, and more motivation to pursue careers they really want. So do employees who feel they have high levels of control at the office. They are better at their job and report more job satisfaction.

Another study Achor mentions showed that greater feelings of control at work predict greater satisfaction in nearly every aspect of our lives and lead to lower stress levels, lower conflict, and lower job turnover.

Remember: How we experience the world is shaped largely by our mindset.

The most successful people believe that their actions have direct effect on their outcomes (internal locus of control), while people with a victim mentality think that their daily events are dictated by external forces (external locus of control).

For example, someone getting passed over for promotion, if they have an external locus, they would think that your employer doesn't recognize talent; that they never had a chance, which subsequently leads to a loss of motivation.

The problem is that people with an external locus not only blame their failures on others, they also – and that's the real problem in the long run – don't give themselves credit for their success.

A person passed over for promotion with an internal locus will just ask themselves what he or she could have done better, and then work on improving that. Or, if they feel they are not valued, they will search for another job.

Believing that our actions determine our fate motivates us to work harder, and when we see this hard work pay off, our self-belief gets stronger. But there are even more advantages:

People who believe they are in control actually have higher academic achievements and better careers. They are much more motivated and happier at work, and experience less stress at the workplace. They also show a higher commitment to their company and better task performance. They build stronger relationships, are better communicators, problem solvers, and more attentive listeners.

Feeling in control is good for your health

In a study conducted on 7,400 employees, those who felt that they have little control over deadlines imposed by other people had a 50% higher risk of coronary heart disease. People who feel like they are not in control over pressure at work are at the same risk for heart disease as people with high blood pressure.

In a study of nursing home residents researchers found out that giving them control over simple tasks in their daily lives, like putting them in charge of their own house plants increased happiness levels and reduced the mortality rate by half!

Ask yourself the following questions:
Who are you blaming for your life's situation right now?
(Your partner? Your boss? Your parents? Your friends?)
What would happen if you stopped blaming others for what happens to you in life?
What would happen if you stopped being a victim of the circumstances?
Is it comfortable for you to be the victim?
What benefits does being a victim have?
What would happen if you stopped suffering in life and took the decision to change it?

5. Change is Possible

The way to happiness goes through change, chaos and through the constant state of feeling slightly uncomfortable. Get into the habit of doing things that others don't want to do, and do what needs to be done regardless of the inconvenience! Most of us think that to change our lives we have to make huge changes, and then we get overwhelmed by the magnitude of the task and end up not doing anything, and therefore, getting stuck with our old habits.

The answer is small steps! Start changing small things that don't require a huge effort, and those small changes will eventually lead to more significant changes.

Be prepared to have fear and doubts as your constant companions on the journey. You might never get rid of them, but you can become better at dealing with them.

Face your fears and do it anyway

According to Paolo Coelho "The fear of suffering is worse than the suffering itself", and Eleanor Roosevelt adds "You gain strength, courage, and confidence by every experience in which you really stop to look fear in the face. You must do the thing which you think you cannot do".

Don't let your fears frustrate you, limit you, or – even worse – paralyze you. See fear as a warning light, not as a red light. I see it over and over again with my clients: Once they start doing what they fear, their fear goes away. Mark Twain knew this already a hundred years ago when he said: "Twenty years from now, you will be more disappointed by the things you didn't do than with the ones that you did."

Face your fears. Ninety percent of them are pure imagination anyway. Illusions! Incredible stories of drama and disaster that will probably never happen and are made up by your mind – "the world's greatest director of soap operas," as T. Harv Eker calls it, to keep you in your comfort zone. The only problem is that great things like development, growth, and success happen outside of the comfort zone.

Fear is your mind's survival mechanism. It wants to keep you safe, and anything that it doesn't know, scares it. This was good thousands of years ago when you head to run from big predators to avoid getting eaten, but nowadays, most of the time it hurts us. Most of the time, behind your fears, there will be great opportunities waiting for you so make it a habit to always ask yourself: "What's the worst thing that can happen to me if I do this?" and evaluate if the risk is worth taking or not.

Be careful. There is also a price for not taking a risk or stepping out of your comfort zone.

Ask yourself "What price am I paying for staying the same or not doing this?" Is it a higher one than the price of taking the risk? This also includes intangible things like inner peace, happiness, health, etc.

Start changing your relationship with fear, one step at a time. Let it warn you and consult you – sometimes, you can even use it as motivation or fuel – but don't let it paralyze or limit you. For example, I used to be totally paralyzed by fear and stayed stuck in my job for five years because of the fear of change or the unknown.

Nowadays, when my mind is invaded by fear and doubts, I think to myself, "Hm, if there are so many doubts and fears, I must be on the right track. I better take action."

Do the things you fear: make that call you don't want to make, send that e-mail you don't want to send, ask that person you're afraid to ask, and see what happens. When you notice fear, have a look at it, observe it, analyze it, but don't believe it. Instead ask it, "Fear, my old friend! What are you doing here again? What's your game? Are you here to warn me or do you want to paralyze me?"

46

What are you afraid of? Failure? Success? Making mistakes? Taking the wrong decisions? Do as Susan Jeffers says: "Feel the fear and do it anyway"! If you want to reach new territories, you have to take some risks and continuously do things that you are afraid of. Mistakes don't matter as long as you learn from them and don't make the same mistakes over and over again. The same goes for decisions – by the way not taking a decision or procrastinating is also a decision!

Be the change

One of my favorite quotes is "Be the change you want to see in the world" by Mahatma Gandhi. It reminds me not to try to change other people, but to always look at myself first, and be an example. Are you trying to change other people? Stop right NOW. It's impossible, you can't help people who don't want to be helped. So stop wasting precious energy and start concentrating on what *you* can do. And that is, to be an example. Be the change you want to see in the world. Other people are like mirrors of us. Things we don't like about them are often things we have to work on ourselves and balance them out. Remember that you are only responsible for your own behavior. Be an example. That's all you have to do.

You cannot change others. The only thing you can do is accept them as they are and be the best example and person that you can be. Are you complaining about your partner, colleagues, or spouse? Be the best colleague or spouse possible! Are you complaining about your employees? Be the best boss possible! Do you want to be loved just as you are? Start with loving other people just the way they are.

Step out of your comfort zone

Yes. Everybody is talking about it. "If you want to change, you have to get out of your comfort zone" or "the magic happens outside of your comfort zone." Yes, I know. Only if it was that easy! It's just so nice and cozy in the comfort zone. By the way...What the heck is the comfort zone?

The best explanation I've heard until now is: If you put a frog into a pot of boiling water, it jumps out. But if you put it into a pot and start heating up the water gradually, it doesn't react and dies by being boiled. (I hope this is just a metaphor and nobody actually boiled some poor frog) Anyway, that's what happens to many people: They are trapped in their comfort zone without even realizing that they're living a life of "quiet desperation".

Your comfort zone is the limit of your current experience. It's what you are used to doing, thinking, or feeling based on your current level of knowledge. It's where we know, most of the time, exactly what is going to happen. It's where you live life on autopilot. It's also where change doesn't happen. So if you want to change jobs, start a company, be creative, get out of a destructive relationship, you have to step out of your comfort zone.

Unfortunately, it really is more comfortable to stay where you are, and your mind does everything to keep you there. If you are trapped in a job that you don't like anymore, you might tell yourself "Well it's not that bad, it could be worse. Who knows, maybe in another job I would be even worse off. My relationship is not that bad. It's going to get better I just have to be patient". This could actually be true. Unfortunately It could also be fear trying to convince you to stay in a job or a relationship that doesn't make any sense anymore.

Steve Jobs had a great technique to get out of his comfort zone: Each day he looked in mirror and asked himself, "If this was my last day on earth, would I do what I'm about to do today?" and if he answered "No" to himself for too many days in a row, he changed. Be careful if you use that technique because once you start asking yourself this question, everything changes. When you step out of your comfort zone, start taking risks, and start to venture towards the unknown, you start to grow. But it starts with the feeling of discomfort and awkwardness, and that's a great sign! That's actually a sign that you are growing and moving ahead. Act in spite of your fears.

Life is a miracle – it always works out in the end. But there is always a price you pay, and it's your decision if you want to pay it and live with the consequences.

The price you pay if you want to get in shape is that you have to exercise and eat healthier. The price you pay for not exercising is getting overweight. If you want more time, the price is getting up an hour earlier or watching less TV. The price you pay for procrastination is anxiety and feeling bad. Choose your suffering wisely!

How does change work? The Power of Habit

A lot of people in this world have made drastic changes, and if the question you're asking is "is change possible"? The answer is yes, change is difficult, but possible. We've established that change is possible, let's get into the 'how' and 'what' part of it. "How is change possible?", "What works?" and "What does change even look like?"

Until 1998, neuroscientists thought that the brain is fixed and that it neither changes nor grows. Nada. You got what you got, and that's it. Thanks to London cab drivers and monkeys, they found out that neurons are plastic, which means they change and that neurons develop and grow. What a breakthrough! Once again I will not tell you how your brain works because I think I'm not qualified for it, and you don't need to know it to make the change. What you need to do is DO.

If you DO something over and over again, it becomes a habit. If you practice, for example, sports or music regularly, your brain changes. The taxi drivers of London had to study the map of London, and their brains actually changed. That was great news because that means everyone can change.

There are two types of change: The gradual and the acute approach.
The gradual approach is like water dripping on stone. This is the healthy kind of change, the real change, and the change that takes time. This is

the fun change where you enjoy the journey and the process of getting there.

The acute approach would be the sledgehammer. This process doesn't take as much time as the gradual process, but it still takes time. Even the acute change is not a quick fix.

And let me tell you one thing right now: There is no quick fix. If somebody is telling you that there is a quick fix…, take a step back, slowly turn around, and run in the other direction!

The founder of Positive Psychology and probably the biggest expert in the field, Martin Seligman brings it to the point dramatically: "The belief that we can rely on shortcuts to gratification and bypass the exercise of personal strengths and virtues is folly. It leads to legions of humanity who are depressed in the middle of great wealth and are starving to death spiritually."

So many people want to change their lives, but they don't want to do anything. They want the quick fix, but the quick fix doesn't exist, so they give up. If only they could have patience and work consistently and persistently to make that change, they would succeed. Like my client, Mary who lost 37 kg (74 lb.) in 15 months after I convinced her that losing 37 kg in 2 months is not only unrealistic but also unhealthy, or my client John who was totally stressed and on the edge of a serious health problem but within 6 months got his life under control, and now has more time than ever, or Petra who tripled her income in 9 months, working consistently like water dripping on stone. Change takes time.

When Stephen Covey looked at success literature of the last 200 years, he found that until the 1930s, self-help was about character change, slow change, changing who you are from the inside. It was about struggling, hard work, failing and getting up again, going through inevitable hardships, and changing step by step; slowly, gradually. Self-help from the 1930s onwards was only about the quick fix, "fast", "do it now", and "easy".

What we see now is what Seligman found. We see a decline in people's well-being, a lot more depression, and a lot more of anxiety. One of the reasons for this development is that people believe in the quick fix. The 5 steps to happiness, 7 steps to success. They try it. They do the steps. Things don't work out, and they think "What's wrong with me? What am I doing wrong". They start to question themselves, and that could be the beginning of a downward spiral. And the worst is...they're doing nothing wrong because there is no quick fix!

It takes time to change

Why is change so difficult?

Why are 44% of doctors overweight although they know how important a healthy lifestyle is? Why is change so difficult? We all know what we should do, but this common knowledge doesn't make things easier. We all know that exercise is good for us and yet we don't do it.

Without action, knowledge is often meaningless. Another reason why change is difficult is that sometimes you think you want to change, but you don't really want to pay the price for it. For example, you want to lose weight, but you don't want to change your diet, or you want to exercise, but you don't want to get up earlier. So you really have to get clarity on that, and you can get clarity by asking yourself the following questions:

Do I REALLY want to change?
Do I want to improve?
Do I want to change things or character or behavior that I don't like?

Another obstacle is that, sometimes we want to change consciously, but subconsciously something stops us: This could be, for example, that subconsciously you think you don't deserve to have a better life. Or sometimes, you associate a positive trait with the trait you want to change, and then you get blocked because you think that if you get rid of the negative one, you'll also lose the positive one, which of course, is nonsense.

For example:

You think if you are saying no, you are not a nice guy anymore

If you're not grim, you lose your seriousness

If you lose your rigidity, you'll also lose your consistency

If you let go of your perfectionism, you'll lose your drive and ambition

What are you tying in your mind to the characteristic that you want to get rid of?

You can lose your fear of failure and still have drive and ambition.

You can say NO and still be a nice guy.

You can stop worrying and still be a responsible person.

You can stop feeling guilty and still be an empathetic and sensitive person.

You have learned by now that fault-finding has nothing to do with realism.

Changing emotions

Mindful meditation, which means putting your attention to the present moment, is an example of a gradual change. It's also probably the most powerful intervention for bringing about calm and equanimity. It's literally like transforming the brain. Studies show that eight weeks of regular meditation can transform the brain. We will discuss this in more detail in the chapter on mind-body connection.

Tara Bennett Goldman, in her book, "Emotional Alchemy", defines mindful meditation – or mindfulness – as "Mindfulness means seeing things as they are, without trying to change them. The point is to dissolve our reactions to disturbing emotions but being careful about not rejecting the emotion itself." This is what "Permission to be human" is all about. You experience the emotion, you breathe through it. Very often, not always, it dissolves and with the emotional dissolution comes the psychological dissolution of this painful emotion.

An example of an acute change in emotions would be trauma. Trauma changes our brain through chemicals and our neural pathways. An example is PTSD. After Vietnam, 30% of veterans suffered from PTSD, after the first Gulf War; 80%.

The acute positive change would be Post Traumatic Growth (PTG). Yes, this actually exists. PTG happens when you focus on the benefits of the trauma, and, for example, subsequently become closer to your family, appreciate every breath, appreciate flowers, enjoy your friends' company more, and overall, learn from it and grow. It's about benefit finding and sharing. Surprisingly, a lot more people experience Post Traumatic Growth. But most of us don't know about it. If people knew about PTG and that it was common, there would be more of it! Because it would turn into a self-fulfilling prophecy.

Changing behavior

Let's talk about the most important ingredient of change. Changing behavior. Most of the people who take a workshop, training, or seminar become happy, motivated, and leave the seminar with great goals and plans just to become 'the same old' on the following Wednesday. Why? How can we make that change last? There is only one way; by introducing immediate behavioral change. Doing some of the exercises we learned, writing down our goals, taking risks we haven't taken before, and so on. This is the real and only secret to change: Behavioral change.

A class, a book or a workshop can introduce a change in your attitude. BUT IF YOU DON'T FOLLOW UP WITH BEHAVIOR, YOU WILL GO BACK TO WHERE YOU WERE BEFORE. If you only go to a workshop, you can have an "Aha" moment, but if you don't follow up with actions afterward, nothing will happen.

Attitudes influence behavior, but behavior also influences attitude. And not only that, behavior is actually more powerful; actions are always more powerful than words

If you have a certain behavior before a class or a workshop, all the class/workshop can do is change your attitude towards a certain thing, but if it doesn't match with your behavior after the class, the attitude is going to be pulled down to where it was before, and that's why on the following Wednesday, you are the 'same old' you were before.

The impact of behavioral change is so strong that prisoners of war writing about the good things of communism to their prison mates and friends actually changed their attitude towards communism.

That's why you can "Fake it till you become it." You can fake a smile to get a happiness boost; you can fake your body posture and body language to become more self-confident with time. Your behavior WILL affect your attitude. Walk with your head up, walk straight, walk like a self-confident person, and you will become more self-confident. Very often, behavioral change is gradual.

The acute change of behavior is about coping, taking risks, coming out of your comfort zone, and doing the uncomfortable.

We can talk about something all day long, we can think about something all day long, and nothing will happen UNLESS we bring about real actual behavioral change! Real actual behavioral ACTION

Tal Ben-Shahar mentions a fabulous study, which I wish I had taken part in thirty years ago:
Shy heterosexual men were told to take a test. They had to wait in a waiting room and were told that somebody would come and get them. In the waiting area, there was a woman waiting with them. These shy heterosexual men were sitting there for 12 minutes with a woman whose instructions were to start a conversation and to show a lot of interest about what the men were saying, listen intently, and ask questions. Then one woman left, and another woman came in. Same thing. Six times. In total there were six women and a total of 72 minutes of conversation. Then the man went to the experiment. And a day later, the same thing again. Of course – as so often happens in psychological studies – it

wasn't about the test the men had to take. The researchers really wanted to see "What effect would the behavior of the women have on shyness".

When they followed up with the men six months later, they were far less anxious, especially around women, and less shy. A lot of times, they even initiated relationships and started to date for the first time in their lives. And all of this, after 144 minutes of intervention! Who still says that change is not possible?

The only problem was that they had to be debriefed six months after the study was over. Researchers told them that it was only a study and that these women were not really interested in them, but that they were told to pretend.

The fun thing is…IT MADE NO DIFFERENCE TO THESE MEN. By then, they were much more outgoing; they were doing well with women; they were going on dates; and they had started a positive spiral. Nothing breeds success like success. When they started to do well, it turned into an upward spiral. That those women were told to 'seem' interested didn't matter at all. 144 minutes changed their lives.

Self-discipline is overrated

Do you believe that you could be happier and more successful if you had more self-discipline? No matter if you do or if you don't. I have good news and bad news for you.

The bad news first: You can't get any more self-discipline. What you have is what you have and you won't get a lot more of it. Self-discipline has a limit.

The good news is: It's actually not that important, neither for success nor happiness. Self-discipline is overrated. **Most efforts to change – organizational ones, as well as personal ones – fail because people rely too much on self-discipline.** If you change your focus from relying on self-discipline for bringing about a change to introducing habits, you'll need a lot less self-discipline. You'll need it maybe in the first 5 to 10 days, but after that, things will come easier to you and before you know it, the habit is installed.

So how do we know that self-discipline doesn't work?
Roy Baumeister did the following experiment: He made two groups. The first group was in a waiting room. They were told the experiment would start in 10 minutes, and meanwhile they shouldn't touch the chocolate chip cookies on the table because they were for the following group.The second group got the same instructions, but there were red beetroots on the table.

The researchers gave both groups the same, very difficult test. What they really wanted to see is how long the groups persevered before giving up.

The results were astounding:
There was significantly more perseverance in the group that had the beetroots. The researchers concluded that this happened because the "Chocolate Chip group" had used most of their self-discipline in order to not touch the cookies and that proved that we have a limited amount of self-discipline. The question is what do we do with it?

Take for example your New Year's resolutions! Are you keeping your resolutions? Then you are part of the 20% who do so, because a whopping 80% of New Year's resolutions die before the end of January!

On the other hand, did you brush your teeth this morning? Did you have to get hyped up, set a goal, get motivated to brush your teeth? I'm sure it happened automatically, right?
The reason is that New Year's resolutions rely on self-discipline, while brushing your teeth has developed into a habit. A lot of times, what seems like discipline – for example in athletes – in reality, are habits or rituals.

The only way of lasting change is habits or rituals.

Create the rituals of running, 3 hours of not checking e-mails, writing down three things you are grateful for, date night, family dinners, etc. If you don't create the habit, the ritual, time – days, weeks, and years will fly by, and you'll never do the things that you want to do. Remember that this doesn't happen in a day. Give yourself the TIME to create the ritual. How much time? Well...as much as you need.

A lot of experts say it takes between 16 and 188 days to create a habit. It depends on the person and the habit. For example getting into the habit of drinking a glass of water every morning after getting up will probably go quite fast. While getting up in the morning to go running for 45 minutes might take a lot longer. Give yourself at least 30 days and try to introduce one or two new habits each 30 days. That should be it. Go for small successes, they will add up to incredible results over time.

Even the Eureka or "Aha" moment takes time, although it seems like instant change, it goes through various stages:
Preparation (Working a lot, immersion in your work)
Incubation (Doing nothing. Relaxing.)
The "Aha" moment (Under the shower. On the bus etc.)

You relaxed your brain and the idea comes. So afterwards, you evaluate and elaborate the idea. It's of utmost importance to take time for creativity. That's why taking time off sometimes is more valuable than working ten-hour days.

How to create habits?

There are various ways to create new habits. The easiest way to break a bad habit is to substitute it with a good habit. You can, for example, substitute a soft drink with green tea or the sandwich for breakfast with a banana. Another way is putting the new habit in a ritual that already exists. Drink the glass of water or fruit juice before making coffee. Make it as easy as possible for you to do the habit and eliminate all the excuses.

For example:

I always wanted to drink freshly-pressed fruit and vegetable juice in the morning.

First problem: No fruit and veggies in the house.

Solution: Buy fruits and veggies.

I started buying fruits, but it got bad in the fridge because I wasn't up for washing them in the morning.

Solution: Wash the fruit right after buying. Great. Still didn't make the juice. Problem: Making juice and then leaving the juicer without cleaning until the next day made it messy and time-intensive to wash the juicer.

Solution: Clean juicer BEFORE drinking the juice.

And that's when I started having freshly-pressed juice every morning.

Lower the activation energy for habits you want to adopt, and raise it for those habits you want to avoid. If you want to exercise in the morning, prepare your clothes, have your shoes next to your bed and if that isn't enough…sleep in your gym clothes (Yes I've done that.)

Plan where you will exercise, when, and what…

Prepare fruits and vegetables in advance and have them in your fridge, so that when hunger strikes, it's easier to grab the fresh fruit than to go for junk food.If you want to break the bad habit of wasting your time watching TV, unplug your TV or take the batteries out of your remote control and have a book ready next to you on the sofa.

K.D. Vohs discovered in his study that too much choice saps our energy. And we make a lot of choices every day. With every additional choice people are asked to make, their physical stamina, ability to perform numeric calculations, persistence in the face of failure, and overall focus drop dramatically. That's why you see Mark Zuckerberg or Barrack Obama always in the same clothes. They are eliminating choices, so they take better decisions in important situations.

Another way to change your habits is making rules for yourself. For example to check your e-mail only once a morning, or taking only one coffee break.

But as I said before...you can know how your brain works, you can have all the knowledge of how to change your habits, but if you don't take actions, if you don't DO, nothing is going to happen. The key to creating these habits is repetition. Practice the habit over and over again, until the actions become ingrained in your brain's neural chemistry.

Shawn Achor tells us in his book "The Happiness Advantage" (one of the best books I've ever read):
"The key to daily practice is to put your desired actions as close to the path of least resistance as humanly possible. Identify the activation energy – the time, the choices, the mental and physical effort they require – and then reduce them." He adds: "If you can cut the activation energy for those habits that lead to success, even by as little as 20 seconds at a time, it won't be long before you'll be reaping the benefits."
Go for it!

6. The Power of Goal-setting

Until just some years ago, I didn't believe what Brian Tracy said: "People with clear written goals accomplish far more in a shorter period of time than people without them can ever imagine." I was not a goal setter; I just wanted to float.

My only goal was to be happy, which I was...until I wasn't anymore. Since I'm setting goals and writing them down, everything has changed in my life. I have become incredibly productive and a lot more successful than I ever was. I'm calmer and experience a lot less stress. Goals have turned my life upside down. The same will happen to you if you give it a shot. And the best part is that you don't even have to reach all your goals to have a great life, but more on that later.

The problem with goals is that most people overestimate what they can do in a month and under-estimate what they can do in a year. So they set huge goals for a month and then give up, because they couldn't reach them, instead of setting a series of achievable smaller goals during a year that would drive them to success.

In this chapter, we will talk about the importance of goals. From the point of theory and practice, but also how they help us deal with stress. I want to convince you to set goals as a way of life in your personal life as well in your professional life. The mere setting of goals and reflecting on them will catapult you into the 5% group that sets goals, and give you an advantage over the other 95%. Yes, 95% of people do not set goals!

Why set goals?

Science has proven that people who set goals are generally more successful and the main reason for that is because goals make us focus.

You surely know the old saying that goes "if you don't know where you are going, you're unlikely to arrive." Or as Nietzsche puts it "If you have a 'what for', every 'how' becomes possible." We are much more likely to overcome difficulties when we have something to attain.

We've already talked about the power of focus and how it gives us direction. Focusing on a goal brings forth internal and external resources that are necessary to get there, and then things begin to happen inside us, as well as around us. Countless studies show that goals contribute to performance and well-being, and strengthen our resilience (because we focus on the future).

When we set goals, we declare that we 'believe' we are going to get something and this turns into a self-fulfilling prophecy. If you write down a goal, if you believe in a goal, the external circumstances is likely to match that, making it much more likely to happen.

I like the following example that Tal Ben Shahar gives in his classes and courses:
When you go on a trip with your backpack, and you come to a wall. What do you do? You can turn around, or you can take a sledgehammer and try to take it down, but usually, you don't take a sledgehammer with you on a trip, do you? So there is this third option: You can take your backpack and throw it over the wall. What? Why would you do that in God's great name?! Because necessity is the mother of all inventions.

You need your backpack to continue. And now that it's on the other side of the wall, you have no other choice but to get over that wall, whether you have to break it down, find a way around it, under it, or over it. You changed your questions, and suddenly you will come up with solutions that you have not seen before.

When you declare a goal "I want to buy a computer" suddenly you see computer ads all around you, in newspapers, journals, etc. Why? Because you are now focused on it, and that's why you see it everywhere. The same happens when you want to buy a particular car;

suddenly you see it all around. When you come up with the goal of "Buying a new car, let's say, a red BMW. Suddenly you see red BMWs everywhere. They were always there, right in front of your eyes, but before focusing on buying a new car, they didn't exist for you.

Back to our wall…
If I declare and decide that I have to get over the wall, my question changes from "Is it possible to get over the wall?" to "How do I get over this wall?" and this makes all the difference! Asking "How?" opens up opportunities, many of which we might not have seen before. Suddenly solutions are right in front of us. If you want to become happier make the question "How can I become happier" the central question in your life.

Another factor that comes in to play with goals is the power of the word. When we declare something, when we say something out loud, it's more likely to become a reality. Add to this that your goals are really meaningful for you and they are much more likely to become true. Words create an image in your mind, and when you create an image of the goal in your mind, the mind wants consistency. Scientists are not really sure how and why it works, but it works.

So what have goals to do with happiness? Here it comes: Goals that are properly understood lead to happiness.

It's not the goal itself that will lead to happiness – we know that now – but the understanding of the proper role of goals leads to happiness:
In other words, it's not the attaining of the goal that leads to happiness; it's the *having* of the goal that leads to happiness.

Goals and focusing on the present

The role of goals is to liberate us to enjoy the present. If you go on a road trip and don't know where to go, you don't have a destination; you are less likely to enjoy the present because every minute you look around, every crossroads or turn you reach, becomes an important decision. This is stress.

If you know where you are going and you have a sense of direction, then you are liberated. You are much more likely to enjoy the process, the environment, the landscape or the proverbial "flowers on the side of the way". No only that, if you have a clear sense of direction, you are much more likely to be happy.

This also explains why a lot of people become less happy after retirement. They might have been dreaming about retiring for years and then, when they finally retire, they get less happy. Bummer! But why does this happen? Because they don't have goals, they don't have a purpose anymore. The ones who do become happier when they retire are the ones who set goals, like learning something new, taking a class, spending time with friends, taking up a hobby.

The truth is that we need a goal for future orientation so that we can enjoy the present more.

Learn to enjoy the progress

Why are there so many high achievers who are unhappy and even turn to drugs and alcohol? How can it be that people who seemingly have everything – fame, fortune, anyone they want, living a life that most people can only dream about – are sometimes so unhappy? How come they end up in a rehab center?

Here's one explanation:
For years on their way to success, they kept telling themselves "I'll be happy when I get to the top," and when they get to the top, they realize that they are at the top and they are not happy. That's when the problems begin. Everyone, including themselves, has probably told them "Once you make it to the top, you'll be happy" but they are not happy. Initially, when they start acquiring fame, they are happier, but

then they go back to the base level, and they are surprised, scared, and even upset. They have no idea what to do.

We've already learned that happiness doesn't depend on your bank account or status, but on your state of mind. It depends on how you interpret your reality and on what you choose to focus on. It's about having a goal; it's about having a destination in mind, and then letting go, and enjoying the process. The present is your point of power.

A great and very comforting thing I learned while studying happiness through Seligman's, Ben Shahar's, and Achor's work is that it doesn't even matter if you choose a certain path and then you regret it – you can be equally happy on both paths – as long as you have a goal, as long as you are committed, as long you are working on your base level of happiness.

It is important though to choose your goals freely. They have to be your goals – not your parents', friends', spouse's, or neighbors' – they have to be meaningful; and they have to be "want-tos," not "have-tos" or "shoulds."

The best goals are aligned with your personal interests and values, with things you care about, and with your passion. Goals that are not imposed from the outside, by someone specific, by society in general, and nor by your own sense of obligation and duty. It's things that you really, really want to do or achieve and not things that you have to achieve. They come from questions like "what are my goals?", "What am I interested in?", and "What am I passionate about?".

Ask yourself these easy questions over and over again, although sometimes the answers are not easy answers. Sometimes, they are not what you want to hear. Sometimes they are not pleasant. Sometimes you might have to go against the grain, choose difficult or least-chosen options. It might be scary, it might take courage, but these are the important questions. These are the questions that can change everything.

The benefits of these kinds of goals are that they are most likely to make you happier because when we pursue something we care about, it is likely to reinforce the enjoyment of the journey.

They also resolve internal conflicts because they make you ask questions like, for example, "What am I doing?" and "Why am I here?", and mind you, these are always the first ones to pop up when we lack goals or directions.

Write down your goals

Writing down your goals makes a difference. Writing down shows your commitment to your goals and those goals will drive you to take action! They are like the GPS system leading the way. But to be led, first of all, you have to know where you want to go.

When you write down your goals, you declare to your mind that out of the 50,000 to 60,000 thoughts you have per day, THE ONES that are written are the most important.

Writing down your goals helps you to start concentrating and focusing on the activities that bring you closer to your goal, and you start taking better decisions. While you are focused on where you want to go, you are also keeping in mind whether what you are doing at this moment is really the best use of your time or not.

When you look at your written goals every day, you are forced to act, and it helps you to prioritize your actions for the day by asking yourself questions such as "At this moment, is doing what I'm doing bringing me closer to my goals?" It's much more difficult to cheat on yourself if you have it written down than if you only have it in your head. For example, you can tell yourself "I've worked so well on my web page today", but if in your agenda it's written down that you only worked one hour instead of five hours, the story changes.

It's important that you are clear about your goals like "I'm going to increase sales by 5% by December 2017", "I'm going to run 5 miles four times a week by November 30, 2017".

Then break them down into small achievable action steps and make a list of all the steps that you will take to get there. Calculate how long it will take you, and don't forget to set a deadline for each action step and goal.

Don't worry if you don't reach the goal by the exact date you've set; it's just a way of focusing on the goal and creating a sense of urgency. Personally, in the last years, I reached only half of the goals I had set. Still, it has been the best two years of my life, and now I'm working on the goals I didn't achieve last year.

In the exercise at the end of this part, I want you to write down what you want your life to look like in 10 years. When you write it down, I want you to write down what you want, not what you think is possible. So GO BIG! There are no limits to your imagination.

The answers you write are indicative of the direction in which your life is headed. Create a clear vision of your goals in your mind. See yourself as already having achieved the goal: How does it feel? How does it look? How does it sound? How does it smell?

Remember the goals have to be yours, specific, stated positively, and you have to commit to them.

It's also very important that when pursuing your goals, you reward yourself for the effort put in, and not just for the results. Self-punishment is strictly not allowed! Keep in mind that you are much further than you were a week or a month ago.

And above all, remember: The most important thing about goals is not achieving them. It's not going to make you happier or unhappier if you do or don't achieve them. I know it's crazy, isn't it? The most important thing is that goals energize us, motivate us, liberate us, and contribute as a means to the end.

Goals will not save you from failures on the way to success, from hardships, from insecurity, or from disappointments – I repeat, those are normal and inevitable. Meaningful goals will help you overcome these obstacles and keep you going and persisting on your way to success and happiness.

Other useful tips that enhance your goal-setting journey are:

- Put a little card with your goals written on it in your wallet and re-connect 4-5 times daily.
  - It's extremely beneficial to have a to-do list. Put your action steps on it, as well as the time it takes to do the task as and put deadlines for each task.
- Balance your goals (physical, economic, social, professional, family, and spiritual).

Goal-setting exercise:

1) What do you want your life to look like in 10 years? There are no limits! Go big!
2) What do you have to achieve in 5 years to get closer to your goal in 10 years?
3) What do you have to achieve in 1 year to get closer to your goal in 5 years?
4) What do you have to achieve in 3 months to get closer to your one-year goal?
5) What are the things that can you do NOW to reach your three-month goal?
6) Write down at least three things and TAKE ACTION!

Examine your values

It's impossible to talk about goals without talking about values. Not in a moral or ethical way, but looking at what fuels you and what motivates you. Being clear about and knowing your values is one of the most important steps to getting to know yourself better. By knowing your values, you will meet less resistance on the way to your goals if those are in line with your values. Build your goals around those values and make sure your profession – whether it's a day job or a business – is according to your values. You don't have to rush into something new, but you can start doing more of the things you love.

If there is a big difference between the life you are living and your values, this might create suffering and tension. Once you find out what your values are, you will be able to understand yourself and your actions a lot better.

So, one of your most important tasks is to find out what your most important values are. Those that bring you joy, peace, and fulfillment. From the list of values (you can download it on my web page www.marcreklau.com for free), choose 10. You may find that you can group values. Then narrow them down to your top four values.

The following questions will lead you to know more about your values:
When do I feel authentic?
When do I feel like myself the most?
When does the real me come out?
When do I feel the most alive?
What is very important in my life?
What gives purpose to my life?
What am I usually doing when I experience that feeling of inner peace?
What am I doing that is so much fun that I usually lose track of time?
What activities do I enjoy the most?
What kinds of moments bring me joy and fulfillment?
What can't I put up with?

Think of some people that you admire. Why do you admire them? What kind of qualities do you admire in them?

Find your Purpose

"The two most important days in your life are the day you are born and the day you find out why." I love this phrase by Mark Twain, maybe because I took so long to find my purpose in life. One of the most important things along your life's journey and one of the key ingredients to your happiness is the discovery of your purpose, which means doing what you love to do.

If you feel like you are driving without a roadmap or a GPS and don't really know where to go or if you never quite know what you are doing here and why, and you feel kind of lost and empty, then that's a sign that you have not found your purpose yet. And of what I hear and read, we have a whole generation facing this problem, but don't worry, it can be fixed. You can find clues to your purpose by examining your values, skills, passions, and ambitions and by taking a look at what you are good at.

I always tell my students "You cannot hide from your purpose, or at least, not forever. You can deny accepting the "wake up call" when it first comes, you can run away, you can hide for a while, you can distract yourself, but sooner or later you will have to accept your calling and the moment you find the courage to do that, everything changes."

Your answers to the questions "What would you do if success was guaranteed?" or "What would you do if you had ten million dollars, seven houses, and have traveled to all of your favorite destinations?" will lead you to your purpose.

I avoided answering these questions for 17 years. In my case, the answers were the same at age 23 as they were at 40: I wanted to write books, inspire people, and show them that a happy life is possible even if you had to overcome the direst of circumstances. I wanted to travel the world and speak about how we can become happier. When I was twenty-three years old, I didn't dare to assume this role, and I had to take a "detour" of seventeen years full of great experiences, which made me the person I am today. And to be honest, I don't know if I would have finally answered to my calling, had I not been fired from my job. Three years ago, I assumed the role, and since then, things have started falling into place. It sounds jargon, but it's true: once you find your purpose, things will start to fall into place. You will start to attract people, opportunities, and resources naturally, and incredible things will start to happen. Nothing attracts success more than somebody who is doing what they love to do.

Here are some more questions that should help you. Have the courage to answer them, better still write down those answers. And, if you're uncomfortable then nobody else but you can see the answers. Don't skip them. I did that for over 20 years, but when I finally answered them, everything changed! Did you ever ask yourself what your mission, your calling, your vocation is? I'm asking because the big problem of our times is that we don't take the time to think about these questions, maybe because sometimes we are afraid of the answer. I highly recommend you to start asking the following questions NOW.

Who am I?
Why am I here?
Why do I exist?
What do I really want to do with my life?
When do I feel fully alive?
What were the highlights of my life?
What am I doing when time flies by?
What inspires me?
What are my greatest strengths?
What would I do if success was guaranteed?
What would I do if I had ten million dollars, seven houses, and had traveled all around the world?

Purpose at the workplace

What does purpose at the workplace look like? How many people who are following their calling and working jobs they really love, do you know? I don't know many. But it's possible.

When it comes to work, everyone falls into one of these three categories:
1) You have a JOB. Your motivation is your paycheck or your monthly salary.

It's a chore. Most of the time you're not enjoying your job, but you have to do it. You don't expect too much from it and you keep looking forward to the next paycheck, to the weekend, or to the next holidays.

2) Maybe you have a CAREER. Your motivations are money, advancement, and getting to the next stage. It's a race to the top, and you are in it to win it. You want more prestige, more power, more money and you are always looking forward to the next promotion. This is also the typical life of the "Rat-Racer."

3) The lucky ones are in the third group, where work aligns with CALLING:
You have goals that inspire you and a mission at their workplace. For you, work is a privilege. You want to do what you do, and actually look forward to more work. You are sad when Friday comes and get excited on Sunday afternoons because finally you can get back to work again the next day.

Now comes the big news:
The interesting development here is that your happiness doesn't depend so much on the work you do but on your perception of the work. There are countless studies on this subject. A study done on the cleaning staff in a hospital showed that some cleaners saw their work as a calling. They perceived their work as very important for the functioning of the hospital. Talking to patients, nurses, and doctors, they felt they were bettering life at the hospital.

In the same clinic, there were doctors who saw their work as a job. And of course, there were doctors who saw their work as a calling and cleaners who saw their work as a chore.

What I want to say is that there are always positive components of a job and the people who burn out don't see them. In the end, once more, it's you who decides how you interpret your work. What is positive about your work?

So what if you feel burnt out at your job and/or your job makes no sense to you anymore?

You have three options, actually no, when you look closer, you have much more than three options, but for the sake of simplicity of the example let's look at the extremes:

So you hate your job, you're tired of it, it makes you sick, but you hang on because you don't have or see any alternatives. Once you reach this point, you can either leave your job – that's option A; you can stay and become bitter and frustrated – that's option B; or option C – you can change the interpretation of your job, and see if you can find purpose in the current job you are doing. You can choose to perceive your work differently. You can change your expectations towards your job, and also reflect on what you are looking for at your job – whether it's the current one, or your next one.

I was at this place once. Burnt out, tired of my job, seeing no more sense in it, but because of fear and lack of courage, I stayed with the company. One day I had a horrible fight with my boss, which resulted in him wanting to fire me right away – until he saw the worth of my severance package – then he quickly changed his mind and tried to fix things, and I agreed, which financially was an idiotic move and cost me a lot of money.

On the other hand, that day I also found a new purpose in my job. I knew that my days at that company were numbered. I decided to save as much money as I could every month to have savings that equal 12 to 18 months of my salary. Having this amount of savings would mean that I could leave the job and start my own business or have more than enough time to find a new job. Suddenly going to work became comfortable again. I had a new goal and purpose: Saving money.

7. The Ugly Twins – Perfectionism & Failure

Remember the question that this book is all about? "How can I become happier?"

Another step on the way to becoming happier is by being less and less of a perfectionist. Now, if you are a perfectionist, you might think "No way, I can't let go of my perfectionism! This would mean I have to give up my ambition". Think again. It's not. You will probably become even more ambitious.

This chapter is about having a different approach toward the journey of your life, towards each step of the way, and especially towards failure. We will talk about perfectionism. The characteristics of a perfectionist, the consequences, and about how it is possible to be both successful and happy. We will investigate where perfectionism comes from, how to overcome it, and how to help other people overcome it. Paulo Coelho hits the spot when he says "There is only one thing that makes a dream impossible to achieve: the fear of failure." The fear of failure is the number one dream killer because most people are so afraid of failure.

Unfortunately, there's no skipping the pain of failure, because that's inevitable, but we can learn to have a more rational, helpful, and empowering approach towards it. Maybe like Napoleon Hill, who indicated that "Every adversity, every failure, every heartache carries with it the seed of an equal or greater benefit." I want you to come to see failure as a learning experience that is necessary for growth and for providing us with information and motivation, instead of something terrible.

What would happen if you could fully embrace the idea that in reality, failure is a sign that points towards progress? Why not adopt the "Edison Mentality." Edison said things like "I failed myself to success" or "I have not failed. I've just found 10,000 ways that won't work." This is what enabled him to bring many of his inventions to us. The man just didn't give up!

If you have the need, the urge that everything has to be perfect, you are doomed to encounter unhappiness, because, guess what, perfection does not exist. You can come close to it, and that should be the goal, but at the same time, you have to accept that it doesn't exist. The good news is that you don't have to be perfect.

"The important work of moving the world forward does not wait to be done by perfect men" George Elliot

Take a minute and remember. How did you learn to walk? How did you learn to eat? How did you learn to draw? Right. By trying over and over again. Could you have walked without falling hundreds of times? Remember how you ate when you were a toddler? It took some practice to eat as you eat today. As kids, we enjoy the joy of learning; enjoy falling and getting up again. And then it goes away...When does it go away? Where does it go?

It goes away when we get to a certain age and notice that people are watching us. Suddenly, we want to maintain a certain image. Suddenly, we avoid things instead of trying it, because "What if I fail," "What if she says no?", "What if my classmates don't like what I say?" and so on.

And we pay the high price for not coping, and it affects a lot of things: our self-esteem, our confidence, our resilience, and finally, our happiness levels in the long term.

Learn to fail or fail to learn

Remember how you learn. You fall, and then you get up again. You miss and then you hit. That's the way. This is how you grow; this is how you learn; how you become resilient, happier, and more successful. It's trying and failing, trying and failing and succeeding, and trying and failing again. Accepting your mistakes as feedback and learning from them.

As Tal Ben Shahar says: "Learn to fail or fail to learn."

You MUST accept that you will fail now and then. I hope you fail many times, because the more often you fail, the more often you will succeed. It's a numbers game. Edward Hubbard was absolutely right when he said: "The greatest mistake a man can make is being afraid of making one."

Be prepared for failure. Be prepared for the worst-case scenario. "What happens if...?" Careful though, I said "be prepared" and not "expect", as by now you know about the power of our beliefs and expectancies. So in the worst case, you fail. What happens then? You learn. It's not comfortable. It hurts, but you will bounce back again, as you did before. That's it.

I failed more times in the last three years than ever before in my life. I was also much more successful than ever before in my life. It was all worth it. And you know what. You get better and better at failure with every time you fail! It hurts less and less every time. If you want to succeed more, fail even more.

If you've read my book "30 Days" you have come across the following examples. Still - in our fight against the fear of failure, they can't be mentioned often enough.

Here is a story of a famous "failure" who literally failed his way to success:
• Lost job, 1832
• Defeated for legislature, 1832
• Failed in business, 1833
• Elected to legislature, 1834
• Sweetheart (Ann Rutledge) died, 1835
• Had a nervous breakdown, 1836
• Defeated for Speaker, 1838
• Defeated for nomination for Congress, 1843
• Lost re-nomination, 1848
• Rejected for Land Officer, 1849

- Defeated for Senate, 1854
- Defeated for nomination for Vice-President, 1856
- Again defeated for Senate, 1858
- Elected President, 1860

This is the story of Abraham Lincoln, a man we would not exactly characterize as a failure, would we?

Here are some more famous failures:

Michael Jordan: cut from his high school basketball team.

Steven Spielberg: rejected from film school thrice.

Walt Disney: fired by the editor of a newspaper for lacking ideas and imagination.

Albert Einstein: learned to speak at a late age and performed poorly in school.

John Grisham: first novel rejected by sixteen agents and twelve publishing houses.

J.K. Rowling: a divorced and single mother on welfare while writing Harry Potter.

Stephen King: first book "Carrie" rejected 30 times. He threw it in the trash. His wife retrieved it and encouraged him to try again.

Oprah Winfrey: fired from her television-reporting job as "not suitable for television".

The Beatles: told by a record company that they have "no future in show business".

So just do it. Just act. Be prepared to fail. Fail and then learn from it. Remember that, in most cases, the most successful athletes are also the ones that have failed the most, like Babe Ruth or Michael Jordan.

Perseverance is more important than talent, intelligence, and strategy. There is great virtue in never giving up. When life doesn't go according to plans, keep moving forward, no matter how small your steps are. The top two habits that will decide between success and failure, between the real change and staying in the same place, are patience and perseverance.

It's highly possible that before success comes, there may be some obstacles in your path. If your plans don't work out, see it as a temporary defeat, and not as a permanent failure. Come up with a new plan and try again, and try, and try, and try, and try some more. If it still doesn't work, adapt until it works. Most people give up because they lack patience and persistence in working out new plans! Just one thing: Don't confuse this with persistently pursuing a plan that doesn't work! If something doesn't work for long, if you've tried every other option and it still doesn't, then change it!

Persistence means persistence toward achieving your goal. When you encounter obstacles, have patience. When you experience a setback, have patience. When things are not happening, have patience.

Personally, I follow Thomas Alva Edison's recipe for success, and I remember it always when I'm struggling and nearly giving up: "The most certain way to succeed is always to try just one more time."

On a business level that means that that organizations or groups that allow their employees to make mistakes, to fall without being afraid of the consequences are significantly more successful. These are learning organizations, where employees constantly learn and grow and are getting better and better.

There is this story – some attribute it to IBM; some attribute it to Southwest Airlines – of an employee made a strategic error. He cost the company a million dollars. So the next day he comes to see his boss and hands him his letter of resignation. And his boss asks "Why?" and the employee says; "I just made a mistake that cost the company a million dollars" And his boss answers: "No way will I accept your resignation. I just invested a million dollars in your education!"

In his book, Geeks and Geezers, Warren Bennis compared very successful leaders who were very young (in their early 30s) and an older generation leaders (in their 70s – 90s).

There were a number of meaningful and interesting differences between the generations, like for example work-life balance. While being very important for the younger ones, the older ones didn't even know what it meant.

But all of them had at least one thing in common: they all had had at least one significant failure, a real crisis, or a significant loss – losing their job, their identity being insulted, or the loss of a person. Both groups saw this point as a turning point in their life. They made the best of what happened to them. They saw it as a learning opportunity, a learning experience, or a stepping stone.

The characteristics of perfectionism

Perfectionism is closely tied to the fear of failure. Its root is the setting of high, nearly-unreachable standards accompanied by an extremely critical self-evaluation and concerns about what other people might think of us. And while perfectionists desire success, mostly, they are focused on avoiding failure. There is a huge difference between demanding perfection and being a person committed to excellence. It's about your approach towards life, towards the journey, towards the process of getting from point A to point B. It has nothing to do with ambition.

1) Perfectionist   **2)** Person committed to excellence

Which one of the two approaches is realistic? I know nobody who has succeeded with method number 1 because it doesn't exist. There is just no straight line from A to B, it's not realistic. It's a fantasy. And people who have this "plan" are doomed to be unhappy and frustrated in life. It's like not accepting the law of gravity. Many people who think approach 1 is possible are constantly frustrated.

Let me make one thing clear: the second option doesn't mean that we enjoy failure. But the first solution provides us – in addition to not enjoying failure – with the frustration of not accepting reality. In the following table, you'll see the major differences between a perfectionist and a person committed to excellence.

PERFECTIONIST	PERSON COMMITTED TO EXCELLENCE
Defensive (in arguments). Doesn't like criticism. There is something that I'm not doing perfectly well.	Open. Welcoming suggestions and criticism - that doesn't mean he or she enjoys it, but it's an important part of growth and development.
Constantly focused on what's not working (half empty glass). Obsessed with failure.	Glass is half full. Enjoys every step of the way. Even failure is an opportunity.
Overgeneralizes. It's all or nothing. Either I'm perfect or I'm a failure	Realistic: Progress.
No self-acceptance	Acceptance of reality, acceptance of personal failure, and acceptance of self.
There is only one way. There is no room for improvisation or deviation. No trial and error.	Flexibility, spontaneity.
Terrified of failure. From within, but also that others see him/her as a failure.	Failure as feedback, growth opportunity.
It's all about getting to B.	The journey is as much part of the success as the destination.

The consequences of the mindset of the perfectionist are that they only experience, at best, a temporary relief, while a person committed to excellence enjoys the journey and much higher levels of happiness. A person committed to excellence is not just about temporary relief, but about lasting satisfaction. They go through the ups and downs that we all do, but they are also able to enjoy the present day and its small everyday blessings like dinners, free time, reading time, etc.

So the question you have to ask yourself is: "What kind of life do I want for myself?"

The consequences of perfectionism

Perfectionists often waste time. Their mentality is ALL or NOTHING. Either I turn in a perfect paper or none, either I get an A or an F, either no cake or the whole cake, either I write a perfect book, or I write no book at all. Supermodel or overweight. This is a very destructive point of view and hurtful on many levels. Don't get me wrong, there are places and professions where you want perfectionism, for example in an E.R. or surgery, but in many other areas of our life it's not necessary, and when it comes to happiness, perfectionism hurts us. The constant feeling of failure and lack of self-acceptance hurts our self-esteem. If you constantly perceive yourself as a failure, it's nearly impossible to have a high self-esteem.

Because of their fear of failure, perfectionists are less likely to try, less likely to put themselves on the line. Unfortunately, those are two of the main ingredients to personal success and happiness. Further, this constant fear of failure also leads to anxiety and stress.

Perfectionism also harms relationships, because perfectionists, many times, are extremely sensitive to criticism and are on the defensive, or, even worse, expecting perfectionism from their partner. If you expect your partner to be perfect, you'll inevitably get disappointed. This leads to frustration and lack of acceptance of the partner, which usually harms the relationship.

Perfectionism is also the enemy of creativity. When you are obsessed with perfectionism, you are also much less likely to act. That's what makes it also one of the primary causes of procrastination because if we don't act, we don't fail. So in the end, we don't act. Or we never cease to act, to rewrite the book or the paper, because it's not perfect yet. And so time goes by. That's why many people start a book and never finish it.

The sources of perfectionism

We are more likely to get over perfectionism if we knew where it came from.

We are not born perfectionists. As children, we actually enjoy the learning process much more than we do after growing up and start being afraid of failing. Children fall, and they get up again.

The problem is the scheme we internalize constantly reinforce that the destination is the only thing that matters. It's the destination that gets rewarded, while the journey goes unrewarded. We believe we are accepted when we reach a certain destination. Very few times we reward the journey, the enjoyment of the journey and failure. This is the kind of social environment we are born into, we are raised in, and it's tough to change. This massive, ongoing, constant pressure to be perfect is all over the media, we can see it on magazine covers, in movies. It's in the workplace. It's in the educational institutions. We are surrounded by unrealistic models and impossible standards.

How to overcome perfectionism

Well, first of all, and as most of the time, it's about self-awareness. Getting aware of what we want and what we don't want. For example, I don't want to be defensive. I want to deal better with criticism, with failure, etc. How can I do it?

Start focusing on and rewarding effort. Yes. Rewarding ourselves for failures, for even trying, and then try again. A third stepping stone in overcoming perfectionism is acceptance. Acceptance of the outside as well as acceptance of ourselves. You don't have to be perfect. Take my word for it. So accept "stuff" and take action, cope with things, put yourself on the line, and last but not the least, look at your weak points and use them as a tool of growth.

Change it by introducing behavior, like for example putting yourself on the line more, and also by visualization and imagining yourself, seeing yourself and behaving like a person committed to excellence

If your perfectionism blocks you from writing a paper, a book or starting a project, use the technique of the "first draft." Tell yourself that it's only a "rough draft," that you will improve it later (like software companies do with their versions 1.1, 1.2, 1.5, etc.)
This will take the pressure away and help you to get things done.

Another suggestion is to apply the same rules you apply to others, to yourself, meaning "Do not unto yourself what you wouldn't do unto others", or better said, treat yourself as you would treat a friend in the same situation. What would you do if a friend fails terribly, or if they make a mistake? I'm sure you'd be much easier on them than you are on yourself, right? Start doing unto yourself what you do unto others. Accept failure in yourself the same way as you would accept it in others, in the people you love. Don't treat yourself differently than you treat others. Be nice to yourself.

Can we help others to overcome perfectionism?

This is a highly difficult task. The will to change has to come from within. Many of us learn it the hard way: you can't help people that don't want to be helped. They actually have to want to change. And always remember, change takes time and doesn't happen overnight.
What you can do is, be an example. If you can change, if you can become a person committed to excellence, a person who enjoys the journey, if you can celebrate even failures, even falling once in a while, then my friend you are leading by example.

People will always rather do what you do than do what you say. Share your experiences. Tell stories about it. Reward effort, reward the journey, reward the attempt saying "What a great attempt, we will get much better next time".

How to deal with perfectionism

Apart from the ways of dealing with perfectionism that we so far talked about, here are some more possible solutions:

Acceptance or what Tal Ben Shahar calls the 'Permission to be human': Accepting emotions; accepting that it's difficult; and accepting reality. Something has just happened, and I can't change it, but what I can change is my interpretation of what has happened.

Reframing: What's the growth opportunity here? What can I learn?

Distraction. Sometimes it's better to distract ourselves when a negative thought comes up. Analysing too much is not always the solution. Go for a run, listen to music, take a break, and then get back to the subject in question at a later time.

Get perspective: Is this really going to matter in ten years? In a year? Is it worth my worrying and being upset? Hint: Most of the time it won't matter.

Will you be nicer to yourself? Yes? OK then. On to the next chapter!

8. Overcoming the Silent Killer

Overcoming stress

Stress has become a global epidemic. Nationwide polls show that 45% of the students experience at the best US Universities suffer from depression until not functioning, and 94% of the students are overwhelmed, which is the result of trying to deal with too much in too little time.

Feeling overwhelmed leads to stress and anxiety, which leads to a higher likelihood of depression. Doctors estimate that about 80% of our physical illnesses are a result of stress, because stress weakens the immune system. The number one cause for loss of days at work globally is something related to our psychology, whether it's stress or related emotions, feelings, experiences

While conventional psychology didn't make a lot of progress asking the question "Why are so many people stressed?", positive psychology researchers were asking "What are those who are successful and able to lead a healthy and happy life doing?" True. Most people are stressed, but not all of them. Some people succeed and at the same time lead a healthy and happy life. What do those people do? How do they deal with stress?

They set rituals/habits for themselves.
They set rituals/habits for work and recovery.

When researchers studied more, they even found out that stress is not the problem and that it's actually GOOD for us! Stress cultivates resilience, strength, and helps to be happier in the long run! Now that's something you didn't expect, did you? But there is more: High level stress turns our immune system to its highest posible level, speeds up our processing, improves our memory and deepens our social connections.

84

Once again it's extremely important how we look at stress.

Shawn Achor speaks of one experiment with two groups. Group one was told "stress is bad for you", group 2 was told "stress is good for you".

Both groups had a high level of stress, but the group that saw stress as a challenge saw a 23% decrease of the negative effects of stress like anxiety, back aches, headaches, fatigue, burnout.

When you go to the gym and lift weights, you are stressing your muscle, and that's a good thing for your muscle. You lift weights, and two days later, you lift weights again and on and on, and after a year of lifting weights, you probably look like Arnold Schwarzenegger during his best days, and you also get stronger.

So stress is not the problem
The problem begins when you don't take breaks, when you don't give yourself the time to recover, when you go to the gym every day. That's when you tear or pull a muscle on a physical level. That's when you become overworked, and that has psychological, as well as physical effects. The problem is a lack of recovery.

If you want to deal with stress effectively, you need to take breaks now and then. If you don't, you will pay the price for it. On a physical level that means you will get injured. On the psychological level that means you will experience anxiety and eventually burnout and depression.

If you give yourself time for recovery, stress is good for you; it might even be exciting at times. Just now I'm reminded of my crazy, very stressful days at work. The stress was nearly unbearable. I think my gift of totally disconnecting after walking out of the office and re-connecting the next day just 5 minutes before entering the office might have saved me a lot of trouble.

A good trick is to change the way you work. One of the most effective and efficient methods is working in time blocks, meaning work hard and focused for 60 to 90 minutes and then take at least 15 minutes for recovery. You could meditate, listen to your favorite music, have lunch mindfully, or do a bit of yoga. Try it. Experiment with it. If you organize your day like this, you'll have more energy, become more creative, more productive, and a lot happier

Of course, you should also maintain flexibility. You can work for two hours straight and then take a one-hour break. When I'm in the flow, I sometimes manage to work with full concentration for four hours, and then I'll take a two to three hours break for lunch, a walk on the beach, and a power nap, and sometimes, maybe, I even treat myself to a chapter of A Song of Ice and Fire.

Organize your day similar to what I just described, take at least one day off per week and always get a good night of sleep, and last, but not the least, take vacations regularly.

The problem is that we are constantly on the run, which makes us miss the beauty that is all around us. That is why we take things for granted and don't take the time to appreciate things anymore.

Stop multitasking

The solution: Simplify. Cut activities. Do less. Fewer commitments. It affects every area of your life. If you have lunch as recovery and you use that time for e-mails and phone calls, then you are not recovering. You are adding more stress. Recovery is just focusing on your lunch or focusing on spending time with people.

Sometimes, as leaders, it's not possible to eliminate multitasking, but it's possible to reduce it. And after reading the next study, you should seriously consider whether you should go on working with your e-mails popping all the time.

The University of London found in a study that when you have your e-mail on while doing concentrated work, it's like taking off 10 IQ points from you IQ, which is the same effect as going 36 hours without sleep. On a side note: Smoking marijuana only reduces the IQ by 4 points.

Nothing will happen if you turn your e-mail off for two to three hours, nothing will happen if your phone is off for two to three hours (unless you are an ambulance driver or a doctor).

Do less and get much more done. Applying this little trick will drastically raise your productivity and work satisfaction. Another way to gain a lot of time is by saying "NO"; to people; to opportunities; and to offers. Simplify, simplify, simplify.

Ask yourself the following questions:
What do I really, really, really want to do?
Where do I need to simplify?
Where do I need to do more?
Where do I procrastinate?

Procrastination

Procrastination is associated with lower levels of happiness, a weakened physical immune system, higher levels of stress and anxiety, and could also lead to depression.

So how can we get rid of it? There are thousand of books written on it. To simplify, here are six ways to overcome procrastination:
1. Push: Tell yourself you are going to stay at least 10 minutes on the task at hand. A lot of times we think that we have to be inspired to start working. That's not true. Most of the times we first need to start working to become inspired and "Just do it".
2. Reward yourself for a task done: Watch your favorite series. Go for a walk.
3. Go public: Set dates, deadlines, and tell it to your friends or on social network sites.
4. Have a team approach: Work with other people. (It's not right for everyone, but it helps most people).

5. Write: Write down your goals, plans, lists, and start working on them.

6. Permit yourself to recover: Procrastinate on purpose, you are not a machine.

If you want more tricks on time management or productivity, you can find an entire collection of them in my book "The Productivity Revolution" which is available on Amazon.

9. Raising Your Self-Esteem

Self-esteem. I actually wanted to write an entire book about it, and I probably will. Nathaniel Branden says that "of all the judgments we pass in our life, none is as important as the one we pass on ourselves."

When I analyzed the challenges my clients had when they come to me, the origin, most of the time, is a lack of self-esteem. Many of the things we talked about in this book like healthy relationships, happiness, benefit finding, benefit creating, depend directly on your self-esteem. And so does not getting the raise you're waiting for, the limits you set for others, how much you value your time, and much more.

Once again, it's not about asking "Do I have high or low self-esteem?" but "How can I enhance my self-esteem?" And this is where it gets interesting: Sometimes, people associate too much self-esteem with arrogance, conceit, and narcissism. That's totally wrong. Arrogance or narcissism are not signs of too much self-esteem, on the contrary, they are signs of a lack thereof.

Definitions of self-esteem:

Albert Bandura, one of the experts on self-esteem, defines it as how people evaluate themselves. "Those who express a sense of unworthiness are said to have low self-esteem or the person who is to express self-pride are said to hold themselves in highest esteem." Self-esteem is "The judgment and feelings about the self".

Stanley Coopersmith defines self-esteem as "an evaluation that an individual makes and customarily maintains about himself. It expresses an attitude of approval or disapproval and states the extent to which an individual believes himself to be capable, significant, successful, and of worth. In short, self-esteem is a personal judgment of worthiness that is expressed in the attitudes an individual hold towards himself". Self-esteem is about the attitude you have towards yourself. It's your evaluation of yourself. "The disposition to experience oneself as competent to cope with the challenges of life and as worthy of happiness." as Nathaniel Branden states.

Feeling competent and worthy. Both are important. You need both to have a healthy self-esteem. If you lack one of them, your self-esteem will be low. The evaluation or judgment about ourselves affects every area of our life.

Self-esteem is essential, yet when we look around us or inside of us, there is room for improvement, isn't it? It's constant work, same like working on gratitude, goals, and so on. When I work with my coaching clients I always also automatically work on self-esteem, because when the self-esteem is high, problems and obstacles tend to disappear.

The benefits of self-esteem:

High self-esteem means high levels of resilience. You'll be better at dealing with difficulties, anxiety, depression, and with the inevitable hardships that accompanies it all.

All your relationships will improve, no matter if it's romantic relationships, friendships, or blood relationships. People with high self-esteem also show higher emotional intelligence.

And last but not the least, there is a very high correlation between self-esteem and happiness. Self-esteem is one of the most important determinants of happiness.

Low self-esteem, on the other hand, causes an unhealthy anxiety. The one that appears for no apparent reason which is also known as self-esteem anxiety. But that's not all... low self-esteem can also cause depression and many psychosomatic symptoms including insomnia, or getting sick because the immune system is weaker.

Nathaniel Branden considers self-esteem as "the immune system of consciousness" because when we have high self-esteem, we are more resilient psychologically. Remember, a strong immune system does not mean we never get sick. It means we get sick less often and when we get sick, we recover quicker.

When Bednar and Petersen studied if there was an underlying cause for most psychological disorders and what it was, they came up with one single thing: Self-esteem.

Further, they found out that self-esteem is critical in understanding many of the behavioral and emotional problems and also in treating most – not all – of them. And that doesn't just apply on an individual level, but also on the societal level.

As a matter of fact, in the nineties, there was a California task force by the government that coined self-esteem as a social vaccine, because they found that low self-esteem is associated with substance abuse, teen pregnancy, school dropouts, violence and crime, while high self-esteem, on the other hand, helps to overcome these social ailments.

Critics

But there are also critics: Often, self-esteem is equated with arrogance and conceit. If you take a questionnaire on narcissism, for example, a lot of times, those who are high on narcissism will also score very high on self-esteem. Now, wait a minute, a person who is a narcissist, who is arrogant doesn't have high self-esteem, do they? We all know that. It's common sense. Someone who walks into a room showing off, bragging, looking like a peacock, probably doesn't have high self-esteem. In fact, this behavior is the exact opposite of a healthy self-esteem. People with higher levels of self-esteem are mostly humble and don't need to constantly show off.

Unfortunately, when we measure self-esteem today, we still depend on questionnaires and if you ask a narcissist "Do you have high self-esteem? " The answer will, of course, be yes.

Most questionnaires are just not sophisticated enough to differentiate between true self-esteem and pseudo self-esteem (the pretense of self-belief and self-respect).

Another critic is that high self-esteem leads to unrealistic evaluation of reality, and that ultimately hurts us. Tal Ben Sahar tells us about an article published in TIME Magazine about a standardized math test that was given to 13-year-olds in six countries. Koreans did the best, Americans did the worst, just after Spain, Ireland, and Canada. But that's not the bad news. The bad news is that the kids were shown the statement "I'm good at mathematics". 68% of Americans agreed to that statement. So while they are bad at maths, they obviously have learned the lessons of the newly-fashionable self-esteem curriculum, wherein kids are told to feel good about themselves

For the longest time, it was "fashion" for teachers to give indiscriminate praise. They thought they were raising the self-esteem of their students by telling them how terrific, how wonderful, how great they were. The problem is that indiscriminate praise doesn't help in the long run. It reduces the student's motivation to work, makes them unrealistic, and actually makes them less happy than they potentially could have been. To build self-esteem, we have to understand its true nature. It's NOT a product of empty reinforcements like "Oh you are wonderful. You are terrific". Self-esteem has to be distinguished from pseudo self-esteem, from the pretense of self-efficacy and self-respect without the reality. Pseudo self-esteem is not self-esteem; it's narcissism and detachment from reality. Real self-esteem is founded in reality, in actual performance, in actual success, and in actual practices. And yes, you probably saw it coming, it's the product of effort and hard work.

More criticism:

A lot of research shows that people with high self-esteem are more generous, more benevolent towards others, and they are generally good. That's good news!

However, there is also a lot of research that shows exactly the opposite: People with high self-esteem show antisocial behavior, especially toward people close to them. Self-esteem has been associated with being aggressive and uncooperative.

What's going on here?

How to cultivate self-esteem

Nathaniel Branden shows us six practices that are essential for cultivating self-esteem:

1. Integrity: There has to be a match between what we say and what we do, the little things and the big things. When we communicate but don't follow up on what we say, we are mainly communicating to ourselves: "What I say is not important. It doesn't matter". Every time we do this, our self-esteem takes a hit. So if we do it very often, our self-esteem suffers a lot.

2. Self-awareness: Know yourself. Knowing yourself is the beginning of everything.

3. Having a purpose: Have a calling. Have self-concordant goals.

4. Taking responsibility: No one is coming. No excuses. No blaming. No complaining.

5. Self-acceptance: You don't have to be perfect. It's impossible. Give yourself the permission to be human on a daily basis

6. Self-assertiveness: Say no or yes when it's appropriate, stand up for what you believe in. Draw a line in the sand that can't be crossed.

Based on the work of Lovinger, Maslow, Carl Rogers, and Nathaniel Branden, Tal Ben Shahar divided self-esteem into three parts, examining it under the viewpoints of worthiness and competence.

1) High dependent self-esteem (everybody has a bit of it. The question is the degree)

2) Independent self-esteem

3) Unconditional self-esteem

	Worthiness	Competence
High dependent self-esteem	They enjoy and need appraisal. Their life is constantly affected of what other people think and say. They take other people's evaluation as the sense of self they have. They are primarily motivated by what other people say. They choose the job with the highest social status, the highest prestige. They choose a partner that they think most people would approve of. They make important decisions based on other people's approval or disapproval. They are afraid of criticism.	Their feeling of competence comes through comparison. (How am I doing relative to other people?). If they do better than others on a test or in a job, they feel great. If others do better than them, they feel bad.
Independent self-esteem	They value themselves according to their own standards. They are self-determined. (They determine how good a book they wrote is). They take into consideration what other people are saying, but at the end of the day, they are the ones who decide. They look for criticism as feedback.	Their feeling of competence doesn't come from comparison to others but comparison to their past selves (Have I improved?). They are mostly focused on the self.

Unconditional self-esteem	No evaluation. They are confident enough not to be engaged in evaluations.	Interdependent. They don't compare themselves. They are in the state of being. Comfortable in their own skin.

Over time, your self-esteem evolves. It takes time to become a "third level," self-actualized individual. It doesn't happen overnight. It takes work: Self-Awareness, falling and getting up again, and learning from failure. It takes learning to accept oneself, being open, being vulnerable and making mistakes. It takes being human. It's a process. It takes time.

The importance of independent self-esteem?

Think about it. The worst atrocities throughout history were conducted by people who were conforming, obedient to authority, and racist or of ethnocentric beliefs and behaviors. A person with high dependent self-esteem is much more likely to be obedient to an authority figure because they are seeking approval. They need that kind of charismatic leader who tells them "you are the best, you are superior." The root of this is low self-esteem. The feeling of "I'm not good enough. I need to compare myself to others." People with a high, independent self-esteem have less need for comparison, as well as less need to conform.

When we cultivate self-love, we cultivate self-esteem. That's when we are most likely to be emphatic and love others. Love your neighbor like you love yourself or love yourself like you love your neighbor. You are the standard of how you evaluate others and very often, not always, your behavior towards others mirrors your behavior towards yourself.

Another reason is that people who have a strong dependent self-esteem will always follow the road that has already been taken, while individuals with a high independent self-esteem follow the road less traveled and think outside the box. They think "What do I really, really want in my life?"

People with independent self-esteem are committed to continuous learning, have higher happiness levels, and a calmer sense of being. They don't have to constantly prove themselves to others. Instead of looking for approval, they say "Let me express myself. Maybe they won't like me, and that hurts. But that's ok. I'm resilient. I'm strong. I can deal with it."

Melissa Christino found a connection between independent self-esteem and happiness and flow: People with high independent self-esteem were more likely to experience flow. While Tal Ben Shahar found that narcissism is connected to high dependent self-esteem.

People with high independent self-esteem are generally much more open, cooperative, generous, and less likely to be perfectionistic

Michael Kernis examined the concept of self-esteem stability and found the following:
"We can predict whether a person will be hostile or generous, whether their self-esteem over time will be higher or lower. It's not self-esteem per se. It's the stability of their self-esteem."

People with unstable self-esteem were more likely to be hostile. People with stable self-esteem were more likely to be generous and benevolent. Dependent self-esteem was associated with instability; independent self-esteem was associated with stability.

Remember that behavior changes attitude!
We pay a high psychological and emotional price whenever we lie, cheat, or are dishonest. Be very cautious about your conversations. Are you just saying things to impress? Things that are not authentic? When we tell the truth, the message we communicate to ourselves is that our words are worthy, our words are important. We matter. When we tell lies or when we are about impressing constantly we are saying I'M NOT GOOD ENOUGH AS I AM. I need to be someone else so that the other person likes me", and our self-esteem and self-confidence take a hit.

How do we enhance our self-esteem?

So how do you improve your self-esteem? Most of the things we already talked about automatically increase self-esteem. For example physical exercise, or finding out what you really, really want in life. Following your passions, your purpose. Answering questions like "What would you do in a world where no one would know what you are doing?" "Where do you see yourself in 10 years from now?" "What's important for you that you would do regardless of other people's approval?" Do you notice that it's always the same questions that come up? The earlier you respond to them, the better.

Another important thing that will enhance your self-esteem is moments of reflection.

If you want high self-esteem, then you have to behave like a person with high self-esteem! Self-esteem, as so many other things, is simply an attitude. It's the attitude you have towards the self. So look for role models and learn from them. Walk like a person with high independent self-esteem, talk like a person with high independent self-esteem, feel like a person with high independent self-esteem. Practicing mindfulness or meditation will also enhance your self-esteem

10. Habits to Boost Your Self-esteem

Stop being so hard on yourself

Don't fall into the habit of self-criticism because of past mistakes or because things didn't work out as you wanted them to. Why? Because it doesn't serve you at all. It's time that you accept that you are not perfect! You never will be, and the best thing is YOU DON'T HAVE TO BE! Stop being so hard on yourself! This is one of the top reasons that prevent people from living a happy and fulfilled life.

A lot of the misery we have in our life is because we subconsciously think we have to punish ourselves for something. It's time to leave the habit of exaggerated self-criticism and self-punishment behind.

You're doing the best you can. This doesn't mean you should stop analyzing your mistakes. It means, you should correct them if you can; and if you can't; accept them, let go, and promise yourself not to repeat them. It only becomes a problem if you keep repeating the same mistakes over and over again.

So here is the magic recipe. It's not for sale at any pharmacy, and it's free! Ready?

1) Accept yourself as you are.
2) Forgive yourself and love yourself.
3) Take extremely good care of yourself.

That's it! Easy, isn't it?

Raise your standards

You teach people how to treat you by what you allow. Expect and demand a lot from yourself, but also from those around you. If you really want to make a change in your life, you have to raise your standards.

Have a zero tolerance policy for mediocrity, procrastination, and behavior that impedes your best performance!

Your standards could be, for example, to always tell the truth, to always be punctual, to really listen to people until they are finished, and so on. Hold yourself to high standards and – what is of the same or even more importance – set boundaries for those around you! Boundaries are things that people simply can't do to you, such as yelling at you, making stupid jokes around you, or disrespecting you.

Communicate clearly and make it a habit to address anything that bothers you on the spot. Remember what the proverb says: "In the right tone, you can say everything, in the wrong tone; nothing. The key is to find the right tone". Practice saying things in a neutral tone of voice like you'd say "The sun is shining."

If somebody oversteps your boundaries, inform them: "I didn't like that comment" or "I don't like you talking to me in that tone." If they go on, request them to stop: "I ask you to stop talking to me like this." By now, most people should get it, but there are always one or two that don't. If that happens, then insist: "I insist that you stop talking to me in that way." If all three steps don't help, then leave! Walk away neutrally stating "I can't have this conversation, while you are _____. Let's talk later".

Self-love is #1

I said it before: Love yourself like your neighbor! A lot of times you see the good in others and fail to see it in yourself! That stops NOW. From now on, when you make a mistake – before beating yourself up – think of how you'd react if a friend or a loved one would have made that mistake. I'm sure in most cases you are much more understanding and forgiving to them than to yourself.

The most important relationship that you have in this life is the one you have with yourself!

If you don't like yourself, how can you expect others to like you? How can you expect to love others if you don't love yourself first?

Accept yourself as you are. You don't have to be perfect to be great. Learn to spend time with the most important person in your life – YOU. Enjoy going to the movies with the best company you can imagine: YOU! French writer and philosopher Blaise Pascal says "All of humanity's problems stem from man's inability to sit quietly in a room alone." Get comfortable with spending some alone time. Find a place where you can disconnect from the fast-paced everyday life. It can't be mentioned often enough: Accepting yourself is the key element of your well-being.

Recognize your value as a person. Know that you earn respect. If you make a mistake, don't beat yourself up over it, accept it, and promise yourself to do your best and not repeat it. That's it. There is absolutely no use in beating yourself up about something that you can't change.

Be selfish! What? What am I saying? Yes, you read right: Be selfish! I don't mean in an egocentric way, but by being well within yourself so that you can transmit this wellness to your whole environment. If you are not well within yourself, you can't be a good husband, wife, son, daughter, or friend. But if you feel great, you can transmit these feelings to your whole environment and everybody benefits.

Live your own life

"Your time is limited, so don't waste it living someone else's life. Don't be trapped by dogma, which is living with the results of other people's thinking. Don't let the noise of other's opinions drown out your own inner voice. And most importantly, have the courage to follow your heart and intuition. They somehow already know what you truly want to become. Everything else is secondary." This Steve Jobs quote already says everything. It's difficult to add something to his wise words. Live the life you want and not the life other people expect of you. Don't worry about what your neighbors or other people think of you, because if you care too much about what they say, there will be a moment when you don't live your own life anymore, but the life of other people. Listen to your heart. Do the things you want to do, and not necessarily those things that everybody else does. Have the courage to be different!

Become a receiver

Accept compliments, gifts, and things with joy, this is also the secret to getting more of what you want. If you get a present and you say "Oh, that's not necessary", you are taking away the joy of gifting from the other person, and the same thing goes for compliments. Take a closer look at this behavior. Is there a hidden feeling of "I don't deserve this," or "I'm not worth it" behind the "That's not necessary?"

There is no need for justification. Don't diminish other people's pleasure of giving. Just say "Thank you!" Practice your "receiving skills." If somebody compliments you, accept it graciously with a "Thank you." Own it. Don't return it.

You may say: "Thank you! I'm happy you feel that way!", and let the other person enjoy the experience. It will help you a lot and take your self-esteem to a whole new level if you manage to eradicate the following behaviors:
• Rejecting compliments.
• Making yourself small.
• Giving credit to others although you have earned it.
• Not buying something nice because you think you don't deserve it.
• Looking for the negative if someone does something good for you.

Invest in yourself

The best thing you can do for your further personal and professional growth is to invest in yourself. Commit yourself to becoming the best person you can be. Invest in training, books, CDs, and other ways of personal development. Stay curious and eager to learn new things and better yourself.

There are so many possibilities: you could partake in some sort of training that improves your negotiation skills, time management, financial planning, and much more. In a two or four-hour workshop you can learn powerful strategies or tools that can transform your life.

My best investments in myself ever was hiring coaches and mentors. They helped me to get unstuck, get clear about what I really want from my life, and change my relationship with fear completely.

You can also start in a less-expensive way by reading more or listening to a learning CD or a course. I made it a habit to read at least one book a week, buy a new course every two months, and sign up for at least two seminars a year. What are you going to do? Remember that baby steps count too.

Be authentic

Did you notice that some of the most successful people are the ones who are authentic? They are not playing any roles. They are who they are. They know their strengths and their weaknesses. They have no problem with being vulnerable and taking responsibilities for their mistakes. Neither do they fear the judgment of others. They put themselves on the line. They cope instead of avoiding. They are incredibly humble and show a great deal of integrity

Don't let the world tell you who you are supposed to be, and don't play any roles. Stop thinking about what others want from you, or might think of you, and permit yourself to be your authentic self. The rewards are awesome! Funnily enough, you will notice that the more you are yourself, the more people will be attracted to you. Try it out!

Honor your past achievements

Oprah Winfrey is totally right. "The more you praise and celebrate your life, the more there is in life to celebrate." This is one of my favorite exercises to boost my clients' self-confidence (and my own).

We are always so centered on the things that don't work so well that we forget what we have already achieved. I'm sure that you have fantastic achievements in your life, and in this chapter you will become aware of those past successes, and use them as fuel to achieving your goals and future successes. So the big question is: What great things have you accomplished in your life so far?

You put yourself through college, traveled the world, have a great career, have lots of great friends. Maybe you lived abroad for a while all on your own. Or maybe you have overcome a terrible childhood or major personal setbacks. Maybe you raised wonderful children. Whatever challenges you've overcome or successes you have achieved—now is the time to look back and celebrate them.

Remember the chapter on focus? In this case, it means that the more you recognize and acknowledge your past successes, the more confident you'll become. And because you are concentrating on achievements, you will see more opportunities for success.

Make your list. Remind yourself of your past successes. Pat yourself on the shoulder and say to yourself "Well done!". Get into the same state that you were in, see the success once again in your mind, and feel the same feeling you had then.

Stop for a moment now. Take five minutes, take a pen and a piece of paper and list down all the biggest successes you've achieved in your life. Come on. Do it NOW.

Are you done? Then read them out loud and allow yourself to feel fantastic for what you have accomplished. Do this various times a day. It will do wonders for your self-esteem. It did for mine.

Listen to great music (Yes, it's important)

A straightforward way to feel happy instantly is to listen to your favorite music. Make a soundtrack of your all-time favorites and listen to them, dance, sing. It might feel stupid at first, but doing this every day will be very beneficial! What are your top 5 favorite songs of all time? Make a playlist on your iPod, phone, or PC and listen to them right now! Do it NOW, and also make it a daily habit.

Celebrate your wins

On your way forward to changing your life and reaching your goals, it's also important to be aware of your progress. Stop now and then to celebrate your wins. Celebrate that you are better than you were last week. Don't let your small victories go unnoticed; celebrate the small wins. Reward yourself: buy yourself something you always wanted, go to the movies, do whatever feels right for you. If you learned new habits and saw great improvement, go on a short trip. You earned it. What will you reward yourself with for your progress so far? Will you have a spa day or a nice dinner? Will you go for a walk?

Have a highlight every day

Don't let routine and boredom crawl into your life. Create things you look forward to after a hard day at work instead of just ending up in front of the TV every evening. Here are some examples:
• Take some "alone time."
• Go for a walk amidst nature with your spouse.
• Take a bubble bath or have a spa day.
• Celebrate something: a good job, family, life!
• Call a friend.
• Take somebody out for lunch.
• Get a massage.
• Go for a drink.
• Go to the movies/theater/a concert.
• Get a manicure/pedicure.

• Movie night at home.
• Watch the sunrise.

Remember to reserve some time for your special moments in your schedule.

Pamper yourself

Self-esteem goes hand in hand with self-worth. Do you value yourself? Do you think you deserve things? Write down a list of 15 things that you can do to pamper yourself and then do one of them every other day for the next two weeks. This exercise is truly miraculous! (Examples: read a good book, go to the movies, get a massage, watch the sunrise, sit by the water, etc.) Once you start treating yourself better, it will do miracles for your self-confidence and self-esteem. These little things will make you feel better, and feeling better will raise your mood and self-esteem. You're sending your subconscious mind little messages like "I deserve this" and this starts an upward spiral.

Unfortunately, this also works the other way round. You don't just lose your self-esteem. It's a slow process. You start denying yourself little pleasures, you stop taking care of yourself, and this leads to a downwards spiral that ends up in a complete lack of self-esteem. Pamper yourself. It will change your life!

Forgive everyone

Mahatma Gandhi said "The weak can never forgive. Forgiveness is the attribute of the strong." Forgiveness is crucial on your way towards success, fulfillment, and happiness. Personally I needed a long, long time to learn this. Why forgive someone if the person did me wrong and it's only their fault? The short answer: It's a selfish act. You're doing it for yourself, not for the other person! This is not about being right or wrong!

This is about you being well and not losing a lot of energy. Anger and resentment and – even worse – reliving hate over and over again are huge energy drainers. Who have sleepless nights? Who is full of anger and doesn't enjoy the present moment? You or the person you're not forgiving? They say cultivating anger and resentment is like drinking poison and hoping the other person dies.

Do yourself a favor and let go. When a journalist asked the Dalai Lama whether he is angry at the Chinese for occupying his country, he answered: "Not at all. I send them love and forgiveness. It's of no benefit at all to be angry at them. It will not change them, but I could get an ulcer from my anger, and that would actually benefit THEM."

Adopt Dalai Lama's attitude towards people who have done you wrong and see what happens. Let go, forgive the people that hurt you, forget them and move on. This doesn't mean you can't put limits on others' behavior or call them out on the spot. But afterward, understand the consequences and let go. Call up people that you have wronged or hurt, and apologize, and if that's too uncomfortable, write them a letter.

Above all: Forgive yourself. When you learn to forgive yourself, it will be easier to forgive others. Just do it. The changes you will see when you manage to forgive others and yourself are amazing.

How to work on this? Here is one suggestion:
First make a list of everybody that you haven't forgiven. Then make a list of everything that you haven't forgiven yourself for. And then – the most important thing – start working on the list.

11. The #1 Predictor of Happiness: Relationships

Let's talk about love. No other topic is talked about so much and also so misunderstood. Scientists found out that close intimate relationships – whether it's with family members, lovers, friends, soul mates – are the number one predictor of happiness. Science has proven that relationships make us happier, more productive, more engaged, energetic, and resilient, and when we have a network of people we can count on, we bounce back faster from setbacks. Thanks to relationships, we achieve more and feel a greater sense of purpose.

Relationships are a natural need. No one can survive and thrive without functioning relationships.

In their research on extremely happy people, Martin Seligman and Ed Diener chose the group of the happiest 10%, and studied them:
They experienced hardships, anxiety, stress, depression, and frustration like everybody else. The only difference between them and the rest was that they recovered faster. Why? Because they interpreted their experience differently because they have thriving personal and interpersonal relationships, either with romantic partners, family members, friends or all of the above.

David Myers says: "There are few stronger predictors of happiness than a close nurturing, equitable, intimate, lifelong companionship with one's best friend".

Relationships make a difference. When you are happy and you share, it enhances relationships. On the other hand, when you go through hardships and difficulty, a strong relationship helps you overcome it

Know yourself

Isn't it funny how we always come back to the same thing? The most important key to everything in our life seems to be knowing oneself. Know how many hours a day is good for you to spend time with other people, know exactly what your relationship needs are, and know how many relationships you need. All that depends on your personal and individual needs. The number of hours you want to spend with other people differ for everyone.

There's no right or wrong on this one, and it doesn't mean you love people any less if you spend less time with them (that's a trap I fell into so many times in my relationships).

If we look at relationships today, it's a pretty dire picture. Two-third of marriages end up in divorce, and the worst of all is that this doesn't mean that the other one-third is just peachy. Often, people stay in relationships out of comfort, out of habit, because of a lack of alternative, or because of a sense of duty. In our times, there's clearly a failure to sustain love over time.

How can we create relationships that thrive?

The first step for accepting reality is understanding what true love really means. Does it exist? It does in fiction and movies. Or better said, it only exists in fiction and movies. In real life, there is no perfect love, and a lot of times relationships fail because we expect perfect love. If your expectations are larger than life, if your expectation is perfect love, then, my dear, you are setting yourself up for failure.

The problem is that "perfect love" is all we read about and all we see in movies. I'm convinced that it's also the fault of the movie industry that some marriages fail. They paint a picture of romantic relationships that have nothing to do with reality, and we internalize it and look for it, and no one can live up to our expectations. I'm sorry to be the one who tells

108

you that Prince or Princess Charming never comes. But I have good news! While perfect love doesn't exist, true love does. True love exists.

Let positive psychology help us identify true love by once again asking different questions, focusing on what works best, and focusing on the few relationships that actually thrive. Traditional psychology counselors or researchers, over the years, have asked: "Why do so many long term relationships fail?" "Why do so many people, after a year or two or five together, end their relationship?" "Why do people stay together although they are no longer okay with it?" By now you know what happens if we only ask these questions: We miss a critical part of reality, and unfortunately, it's the part of reality that can lead to lasting, thriving, and passionate relationships.

Positive psychologists changed the question to "What makes some relationships thrive and grow stronger over time?" These relationships exist. "What makes them successful?" And the most important question: "What can we learn from those and apply to our relationships?"

John Gottman, one of the leading researchers on relationships – who also can predict divorce with an accuracy level of 94% - says "When I figured out how to predict divorce, I thought I had found the key to saving marriages, but like so many experts before me, I was wrong. I was not able to crack the code to saving marriages until I started to analyze what went right in happy marriages."

David Schnarch showed in his research studying the best relationships that those couples not only enjoy spending time together over the years but that the best sex they have in their lives actually comes when they are 50 and 60 years old, and not when they are 18, 25, or 35.

Sorry that I have to be the killjoy here but I think you guessed it already. Unfortunately the majority of relationships are not like that. Mostly because a significant number of people today are in their second or third marriage or long-term relationship at the age of 50 and 60.

So what are the secrets to a thriving relationship?
It's hard work. You need to invest if you want to thrive in a relationship.

Create high levels of intimacy. Maintain passion. Appreciate the good.

One of the key mistakes that I made for the longest time, and I actually was able to start changing it when I heard about this the first time from Tal Ben-Shahar, was that I had a so-called "Finding Mindset" for most of my life. Boy, was letting go of the "Finding Mindset" and learning the "Cultivating Mindset" a relief! It's like a huge weight off my shoulders.

When you have a "finding mindset" you focus on finding the right partner. Big mistake! Finding the right partner is important, but it's not the most important.

The problem with the "Finding Mindset" is that when you go through rough times with your partner, which by the way is totally normal, you start thinking "Wait a minute. Something is wrong here. I must not have found the right partner. I must have made a mistake." This happened to me every single time, and it made the situation worse. And sooner or later the relationship ended.

With a "Cultivating Mindset" that wouldn't have happened, because you rather think: "Okay. We are going through some difficulties, but we are working on our relationship. It's normal. We make an effort to understand each other. We grow together." It's this mindset that makes relationships last.

It's more important to cultivate the relationship than to find the right partner. Don't misunderstand me: It is important to find the right person, but it's even more important to then cultivate that relationship

So why in the world do people have the "Finding Mindset"? Here I am, once again, blaming the movies. They are beautiful, but there is one problem, they focus on finding the right partner. And the actual work starts when the movie ends and the curtain drops. Having a good relationship at the beginning is easy. The honeymoon phase usually lasts through the first year or two. But what happens then? What happens when we see that the partner is not perfect? That's where true love begins, and that's where true love is cultivated.

I always believed that there is more than one right person. Mostly after a relationship ended of course. And come on, we are nearly 7 billion people in the world, it's insane to think that there is only one person for us. It's also not important because true love is not about finding the right person. It's about cultivating the one chosen relationship. It's working together, being together, spending time together, and dedicating one to another. That's how we create the one special relationship. It's a process, and it takes time. We cultivate a relationship not simply by putting on the ring or by reciting the vows, but by doing things together, by actually getting to know each other.

John Gottman found out that "in the strongest marriages, husband and wife share a deep sense of meaning. They don't just get along, they also support each other's hopes and aspirations and build a sense of purpose in their lives together."

How do we sustain love?

1) Create relationship rituals.
We've heard it often: "Love is in the details." Love is not in the three months around the world cruise or the diamond ring. These things are lovely, but they don't sustain a relationship. It's the details, the habits, the day-to-day rituals that maintain relationships. The touch, the gaze, the meal together, remembering important dates, compliments, text messages, kisses, hugs, and appreciating our partner every day. These little details and day-to-day activities make a relationship extraordinary. And you do this by demonstrating interest. Asking "How was your day honey?" "Tell me about..." "What have you just been thinking?", "You look a bit sad, anything I can do?", and listening with empathy. Are you

really listening to your partner? Are you really looking at your partner? Do you really want to get to know them?

And of course, sex is also important for a long-term thriving relationship. A divorce lawyer once told me: "You know, I never divorced a couple that had great sex." And while this might be his exclusive opinion, it is very rare to have a romantic relationship without the physical component. The most important thing also in this department is healthy communication. Very often there is a difference in expectations because there's no "right prescription" of how many times you should have sex to make your relationship work. Once a day? Five times a week? This is a potential source of conflict so communicate with your partner. For you, sleeping with your partner three times a week could be a lot, but maybe for your partner it's not enough. Find out by talking to each other. My relationships improved a lot when I started talking about my wishes openly with my partner instead of hoping they could read my mind about what I desired.

2) Shift from "to be desired/validated" to "to be known"
No matter what kind of relationship – romantic or friendship – the foundation of great relationships is to be KNOWN. You get to deeper levels of intimacy by getting to know each other more and more. We do this by opening up, sharing meaningful things with our partner, opening up and also sharing our weaknesses, our insecurities, and our passions. As Tal Ben Shahar says "A healthy relationship is about expressing ourselves rather than constantly trying to impress".

This is risky because what happens if she doesn't like you? But it's worth the risk because if you express yourself and open up, you are more likely to have a thriving relationship. There is no guarantee, but one thing is for sure: If you just try to impress, failure is guaranteed.
Did you notice that people who take the risk, who authentically express themselves over time attract more and more people? Genuine people are more attractive. It doesn't matter if it's friends or leaders. There is nothing like being authentic. Integrity attracts.
If you only impress, you'll always be asking yourself "Who do they really like? Me or the image?" and this will soon become a self-inflicted torture.

Make an active effort to get to know your partner. This takes time and doesn't happen on the first date.

3) Allowing conflicts in the relationship.
There will always be conflicts in relationships. It's okay. It's normal. All relationships face it. Instead of asking "What's wrong" in the relationship we can shift to "Ok. It's normal. It's natural. Let's see how we can learn from it and grow as a couple". Once again, everything is about concentrating on and strengthening the positive.

By the way, people who have a 1:5 conflict ratio usually have a thriving relationship. 1:5 means one conflict every five positive interactions. People who have a lot less or a lot more conflict usually don't have a relationship that thrives in the long term. At 1:100, for example, it could mean there are some oppressed things. And if you fight all the time it really might be time to part ways.

For a long time, it was thought that you only have to bring the conflicting parties together and talk to solve the problems. That was wrong and frequently made things worse.

The important thing in resolving conflicts is that both parties have a higher common goal together, working together, and supporting one another.

We also have to be aware that there is positive as well as negative conflict. Healthy conflict focuses on a person's behavior, thoughts, ideas and challenge, for example, saying "You mind putting down the toilet seat when you are done?" or "It upsets me to return to a dirty home, we agreed you'd throw away the garbage".

Unhealthy conflict focuses on the person, on the emotions, on who they are, such as saying "You're so inconsiderate" or "You're such a slob, you promised to throw away the garbage. I can't trust you."
When you attack someone for who they are, the person, the emotion it's very unhealthy no matter if it's a group or a couple.

It's of utmost importance to avoid hostility, insult, and contempt.
John Gottman – the guy who can predict divorce with a 94% accuracy rate – talks a lot about it in his research. He predicts divorce based on

whether he sees hostility or contempt when he asks couples about their conflicts.

When there are hostility and contempt, it's a very bad sign. It doesn't always lead to divorce, but it's a bad sign for the long-term likelihood of success of the relationship and regarding the current enjoyment of the relationship.

It's important to keep these insults away, to focus on the person, to validate/appreciate the person and disagree with their behavior or the ideas and their thinking. It goes without saying that the key is to keep the disputes private. It's difficult enough to fight in a relationship; it's extraordinary difficult when embarrassment is also associated with it. Couples shouting at one another, or showing contempt in front of others are on a very destructive, and extremely unhelpful path.

We have to learn to fight better:
Improving the ability to disagree by being more positive, introducing more humor, more affection, more touching, and more talking. This helps to dissolve tension. Stop taking negativity by personally telling yourself "I understand this is part of the growth. We may not be enjoying ourselves now. It's a serious fight. But what can I learn from it." Show more attention to your partner's side. Calm down, understand, and be emphatic. Learn to treat those we love the same or even better than we treat others because a lot of times we treat others better than the ones we love.

4) Positive perception
We have to appreciate the other person and vice versa. I'm sure we've all seen and experienced it: Once we take a relationship for granted, it starts to worsen. Unfortunately, that happens to most relationships. The secret is to always focus on what works. Focus on your spouse's sense of humor, on their support, on how they are a good mother or father, etc. Become a "Benefit finder" in your relationships.

Sandra Murray conducted another one of these remarkable experiments that more people should know about. She asked couples to evaluate each other's strengths. Afterwards, she asked friends and family to do the same. The results were once again mind-boggling:

On an average, relationships of couples that evaluated their strengths on a lower level than friends and family didn't last very long, while couples that evaluated one another's strength on a higher level, who thought of their partner more than other people thought of them, were most likely to succeed over time.

The fact of thinking more of their partner than other people think of them is also called "positive illusions." Only that, it's not an illusion, it becomes a self-fulfilling prophecy!These thriving couples are actually "benefit creating". They are seeing things that are not there or that other people have not seen, and then these things come into existence. It's the Pygmalion effect all over again, this time in relationships.

The importance of asking the right questions and open communication

You remember that when we ask certain questions, we start seeing things that we didn't see before, right? So here are the two most important questions that you should ask over and over again to create and maintain a thriving relationship:

1) What am I grateful for in my partner? There is always something to appreciate, especially in difficult times.
2) What's wonderful about our relationship? What's working? What do I love about him/her? What's good? When we ask what's good, then we perceive it. When we perceive it, we appreciate it. When we appreciate it, it grows.

We have to change our questions to the right ones, focus on the potential of our relationships, and communicate mostly about the positive events we are experiencing.

Which brings us to our next study about positive communication. Shelly Gable found out that the way couples communicate about positive events is a better predictor of long-term success in a relationship than how they talk about negative incidents.

So, when you come home and talk about something positive, a good thing that happened to you, and the way your partner responds is a predictor of the long-term success of your relationship.

There are four ways of responding: constructive vs. destructive and active vs. passive. Out of the four ways to respond, only one contributes positively to the relationship.

Active and constructive: Comprise of enthusiastic support, specific comments, and follow up questions:
"I just got a promotion!" "That's amazing! What happened? Tell me! We have to celebrate. Let's go out."

Harmful responses are:
Passive and constructive responses: "That's nice" "Oh that's great. Mmmh."

Active and destructive: "Oh No! Now we have less time together." "I'm surprised."
The worst:

Passive and destructive: Ignoring the news entirely. Showing no interest: "Mmh. Did you see we got a new flower in the garden."
The only conditions for active and constructive communication are that it has to be win-win and it has to be genuine. If these are given, this way of communication can cause an upward spiral for our lovebirds.

Relationships at work

We spend most of our time at work, so let's look at the influence of relationships at the workplace. A national survey of 24,000 workers concluded that men and women with few social ties were two to three times more likely to suffer from major depression than those with strong social bonds. Another study shows that people who received emotional support during six months after a heart attack were three times more likely to survive.

Good relationships and positive interactions with our colleagues at work lower cortisol, which means we recover faster from work related stress and are better able to handle it in the future. And this is where CEOs should pay attention:
The ability to manage stress – physically and psychologically – is a significant competitive advantage. It has been found to greatly reduce a

company's health care cost and rate of absenteeism. But there is more, these positive social interactions also result in employees being able to work longer hours, focus better, and perform under more difficult conditions. A study of men over the age of 50 that had a lot of stress in their life showed that those who lacked high levels of emotional support suffered from a far higher mortality rate in the next seven years than those who had good relationships and emotional support.

When over 1,000 highly successful professionals were asked what had motivated them most during their career, they ranked friendships above financial gain and individual status, and in a study of 350 people of a financial services company, the greatest predictor of team success was how the members felt about each other.

It's a fact that the more team members are encouraged to interact face to face, the more engaged they feel, and the more energy they have. In short, the more the investments in social connections, the better the results of their work

The best companies already know this and put it into practice. IBM, for example, facilitated the introduction of employees who didn't know each other. Google keeps company cafeterias open well past the hours and encourages employees to see their kids at their onsite daycare center. It's surprising that a logistic company that is all about speed encourages their drivers to have lunch together. Nevertheless, UPS does exactly that.

If employees believe and say "I have a sense of pride in my organization" a company can congratulate itself because these feelings translate into lower absenteeism and employee turnover and increased employee motivation and engagement

The most important relationship at work

The relationship between employee and the boss is the prime predictor of both daily productivity and the length of time people stay at their jobs, because "People don't change jobs, they change bosses."

This is the most important relationship in a company, and it has consequences. A Gallup study found out that US Companies lose 360 billion USD each year due to lost productivity from employees who have a poor relationship with their supervisor.

If people have a difficult relationship with their bosses, it also has consequences on their health: Their blood pressure can spike all over the place, and they are 30% more likely to suffer from coronary heart disease.

On the other hand, when the boss-employee relationship is strong, it's extremely beneficial for the company. And there is proof. An MIT study confirmed that employees with strong relationships with their managers bring in more money than those with only weak ties.

A Gallup study of 10 million workers came to the following conclusion: Those who agreed to the phrase "My supervisor, or someone at work seems to care for me as a person" were more productive, contributed more profits, and were significantly more likely to stay with the company in the long term.

And although the best leaders already know all this, many of them don't put in the effort to reap the benefits of these findings. Either because they don't have the time, or because they feel a loss of authority, or because they just believe that friendship and work don't go hand in hand or as my former colleague Iñaki used to say: "If you want a friend, buy a dog".

It's really easy to create a better work environment. Once again it's common sense.

Greet colleagues, look them in the eye to create rapport and empathy, have a face-to-face meeting now and then, and talk also about things outside of work instead of talking all the time about the project or task at hand. The simple act of introducing new employees to not only to their department but also to other departments has brought tremendous benefits in the long term for companies who do it. And it's not only the new joiners. While you are at it, introduce existing employees, who don't know each other to each other.

I'm not telling you that everybody has to be BFFs at work or that everybody has to like each other all the time. What matters is mutual respect and authenticity. Team lunches and socializing after work are crucial, but relationships have to develop naturally and can't be forced.

Emotions are contagious – negative and positive ones – and they can affect a group of people almost instantly. We notice this in us as well as in others. When we feel anxious or have a real bad day, our feelings will start to creep into every interaction we have, whether we like it or not. And the results, not just our own, will suffer from this.
If you ever sat close to an anxious boss who is in a bad mood for too long, you know what I'm talking about. After a while, you probably felt sad or stressed too, regardless of how you felt initially.

That's why it's so important to have a positive mindset. Science has proven over and over again that positive emotions are a tool in the quest for high performance at the workplace. The happier everyone is around you, the happier you are and vice-versa. The happier we are at work, the more positivity we transmit to our colleagues, clients, etc., which can raise the emotion of an entire team.

This was proven by an experiment at Yale:
During a group task, one member of the group was instructed to be openly positive. The experiment was video taped and tracked emotions of each individual team member before and after the session. The individual and group performances were assessed.

The results were once again spectacular: They showed that whenever the positive team member entered the room, his mood instantly infected everybody around him. His positive mood actually improved each individual team member's performance as well as their ability to accomplish the task as a group. But not only that, researchers also found that the teams with the one positive person infecting everybody with his mood had less group conflict, more cooperation, and, most importantly, greater overall performance.

The more genuinely expressive you are, the more your mindset and feelings spread.

And, read this closely if you are in a leadership position, in a leadership position the power to infect you employees with positive emotions multiplies. If you, as a leader, are in a positive mood, your employees will be more likely to be happy themselves, to help each other more and to coordinate tasks more efficiently and with less effort.They'll also be more likely of being happy and describing their workplace as performance enhancing – two huge advantages in employee attraction and employee retention.

People in positive moods are also better at thinking creatively and logically, at problem-solving, and are even better negotiators.

12. The Power of the Mind-Body Connection

For a long, long time in the western society we concentrated only on what happens "neck up" but most of what happens is "neck down".

In this chapter, I'm going to talk about Tal Ben Shahar's secret wonder drug! As he says, he's not a good businessman, so he never commercialized the drug, and we can get our hands on it for free. This drug has been tested over and over again. And the best is that there are no negative side effects, on the contrary, there are tons of positive benefits:

• It's going to make you feel really, really good!
• Your self-esteem is going to rise significantly.
• Your self-confidence is going to get a boost.
• You will feel calmer and more centered.
• You'll even get smarter.
• It's also going to make you more attractive.

So here it is – the wonder drug:

• 30 minutes of physical exercise 4 times a week
• At least 15 minutes of mindful exercise 6 to 7 times a week
• 8 hours of sleep (+/-) per 24 hours
• 12 hugs a day

If you take this cocktail, you will reap many of the benefits, maybe all, and probably even much more.

One of the first people to understand the mind body connection was John Kabat Zinn. He stated the following: "Perhaps the most fundamental development in behavioral medicine is the recognition that we can no longer think about health as being solely a characteristic of the body or the mind because body and mind are interconnected".

This was a revolution and essentially a rejection of hundreds of years of western thinking. But since then, many researchers have proven him right. They did because they were asking a new question: "How can we use the body to launch a virtuous cycle between where the mind helps the body and the body helps the mind?"

The Magic of physical exercise

We all know the advantages of physical exercise:
- It boosts our mood and enhances work performance.
- It improves our motivation and feeling of having achieved something.
- It reduces stress.
- It helps you feel better and more energetic.
- It keeps you healthy.
- It helps you to lose weight, which improves health, and also makes you look better.

Once the kilos start dropping, there is a big chance that your self-esteem will go up.

The problem is despite knowing this, most of us don't exercise. Let me show you some amazing studies that will hopefully convince you to start physical activity. The most incredible research about the positive benefits of exercise was done by Michael Babyak from Duke Medical School:

He took 156 patients with major depression – people in very bad shape – showing a number of symptoms like insomnia, eating disorders, lack of desire to act, depression, and most of them were suicidal with attempts or thoughts about suicide, and divided them into three groups.

The first group did 3 x 30 minutes of exercise of moderate difficulty (jogging, swimming or brisk walking). The second group was put on medication (Zoloft), and the third group was on medication and asked to exercise. After four months, Babyak got some stunning results: 60% of the subjects were not experiencing the major symptoms of depression any more, meaning they recovered. All groups experienced similar improvements in happiness, which means that exercise proved just as helpful as antidepressants! The medication group took about 10-14 days to get over depression, while the exercise group close to a month, but later there was no difference. Amazing, isn't it? But there is more:

Six months after the study ended, when the participants were no longer given the medication or no longer pushed to exercise they had a look at a look at the relapse rate.

Out of the 60% that got better, 38 percent of the "only medication" group went back and suffered from major depression again. From the third group (medication and exercise), it was 31%. But from the exercise group, there were only 9% who fell back into depression.

This means that exercise is a powerful and lasting mood lifter. It doesn't mean that medication isn't necessary any more, but it means that we should maybe first ask whether exercise or the lack thereof is the underlying reason for the experience.

Don't get me wrong. There are and there will be people who can only be helped with medication, people who can be helped by exercise, and people who need both. But maybe we could try exercise too. Exercise is not a fix-all. However, in most situations, it can help or prevent.

I'd say exercising is like taking an anti-depressant. Tal Ben Shahar argues that it's the other way round: Not exercising is like taking a depressant, because we just weren't made to sit through all day, we were made to run after our lunch or to run away from lions to not end up as lunch. When we don't exercise, our base level of happiness lowers. Exercise brings us back to where we are supposed to be all along.

The benefits of exercising, at least every other day, are countless:

- It increases you self-esteem and lowers stress and anxiety.
- After you go for a run, your brain is most susceptible to creating new neural pathways.
- It improves your memory, meaning that you retain material you have learnt much better.
- You become much more creative.

People who exercise are much less prone to physical diseases; significantly reducing the likelihood of diabetes; reducing by 50% or more the likelihood of heart failure; reducing the likelihood of certain kinds of cancer; and strengthening the immune system.

And if I didn't convince you by now:
You will also have better sex, both men and women. Exercise strengthens libido, and enhances the likelihood of orgasms. People who exercise more regularly have more and better sex.

Before you start your exercise program, remember: Recovery is very important and more is not always better. Funnily enough, the symptoms of overtraining are very similar to the symptoms of under training

Shahar's general recommendation is to exercise a minimum of 3 to 4 times a week, ideally 5 to 6 days for a minimum of 30 minutes at 70% of your maximum heart rate. Four times 30 minutes should be enough. Just listen to your body.

If exercise is so powerful...why do most of the people in the world not exercise?
The three most common reasons are: It's painful, not enough time, and the subconscious barrier.

1) Exercise is painful. It's not comfortable and our mind does not like pain. It tries to avoid pain.

The solution? As mostly, when you start working on a goal: Divide and Conquer. Start walking for a mile, do a 10 minutes walk, then a 20-minutes walk and gradually build it up. Your body will ask for more. If you build it up gradually, it's not about pain; it becomes positively addictive. I've seen it. My friend Marina started out walking for minutes. Five years later, she's running 10k and 20k races. Start slow and your body will ask for more.

If it gets too boring, distract yourself with TV, music, or podcasts. Whatever you can think of. Go running with other people. The number one predictor of exercise and success in the long term is to do it with other people.

2) Not enough time:
One of the first things to go when you don't have time is exercise, while it should be the last thing to go. Exercise is an investment. You might lose 45 minutes, but you gain so much more. Remember all the benefits we talked about at the beginning of the chapter.
Also remember: Don't rely on self-discipline, create rituals.

3) The subconscious barrier:
Even self-esteem or the lack thereof can come into play when we don't exercise. Part of low self-esteem is the notion that we are not worthy of happiness. Subconsciously, we often think: we are not really worthy of happiness and this can become a barrier that stops us from becoming happier. If we think we are not worthy of happiness, we will, very often, not do things that will make us happy. The solution? Like Nike said: JUST DO IT and recognize the importance of exercise on a conscious level.

Harvard Medical School Professor and Psychiatrist, John Ratey said "In a way, **exercise can be thought as a psychiatrist's dream treatment.** It works on anxiety, on panic disorder, and on stress in general, which has a lot to do with depression. And it generates the release of neurotransmitters, norephedrine, serotonin, and dopamine that are very similar to our most important psychiatric medicines. Doing a bit of exercise is like taking a little bit of Prozac, and a little bit of Ritalin right where it's supposed to go."

To finish the chapter on exercise, here is another amazing experiment: Here's what happened when 45 minutes of some form of exercises like running, rowing, climbing, cycling etc. were implemented in schools: Obesity levels went down from 30% to 3% in a school in Naperville, Illinois. Students became more comfortable, happier, and much less susceptible to chronic illnesses, such as cancer, heart failure, diabetes, and their grades went up significantly. Naperville scored number 16 in the world in mathematics and number 1 in the world in science. A great achievement, considering that US schools usually don't score well in international tests.

Exercise was also introduced in inner city schools in very poor areas. In Titusville, PA, grades went from way below state average to 17% above state average in one year after introducing exercise. Another advantage of introducing exercise was that violence disappeared completely as result of it. In Iowa, disciplinary problems went down from 225 to 95 in one year; in Kansas, by 67%. That's no surprise knowing that exercise calms us so we are much less likely to be aggressive.

The Power of Meditation

Meditation has gone mainstream. Maybe you've already experimented with it. If not, I highly recommend it. It's easier than you thought. And in its easiest form, you basically can't do anything wrong. There are various kinds of meditation like yoga, focusing on your breath, praying, sitting meditation, Tai Chi, and so on. All meditations have things in common like focusing on one thing, for example movement, posture, breath, or a flame and breathing deeply.

As I mentioned before, there is no good or bad meditation. It's about being present, being in the here and now, it's also about struggling with being in the here and now. When you lose you focus, simply bring it

126

back, that's how we exercise our mind to be more focused and be more mindful.

John Kabat-Zinn and Herbert Benson studied the world's bets meditators. They directly contacted the Dalai Lama himself to send his best meditators, and the results of the studies were mind-boggling.

First they looked at left to right prefrontal cortex ratio, which is important for measuring happiness. Happier people generally have more activity on the left side of the prefrontal cortex, and less happy people have more activity on the right side of the prefrontal cortex. The meditators had very high levels of well-being and happiness. They were susceptible to positive emotions and resilient in the face of painful emotions. These were remarkable results, which have never been seen before measuring the meditators.

Another thing they looked at was the so-called startle response, something that everyone has, even military snipers. When we hear a bang, we startle. Generally the higher your level of anxiety, the easier you get startled. It's impossible to suppress the startle response. Or better said, it was impossible until Paul Ackerman brought in the meditators and asked them to maintain complete calm. He startled them. And surprise, surprise...there was no reaction at all. For the first time in recorded history, people were able to suppress the startle response.

You know that emotions are contagious. So is calmness. Calmness is as contagious as happiness. Even people who wanted to start a discussion with those people could not get angry.

Now the good news is that you don't have to meditate 8 hours a day for 30 years to get the benefits of meditation.

John Kabat Zinn conducted another experiment. He worked with two groups. The first group started meditating right away, the other group - the control group - was told they will start their meditation course in four months. The researchers wanted to make sure that the control group were people that wanted to meditate.

So group 1 started to meditate 45 minutes a day for 8 weeks. The results were once again stunning: their anxiety levels went down and they were in a happier mood. Looking at the left and right prefrontal cortex, there was a significant difference in the individuals who meditated. So Kabat-Zinn went one step further. He injected a cold virus in both groups and found out that the immune system of the meditators was significantly stronger than those who didn't meditate. Meditation strengthens both our physical as well as our psychological immune system.

And it gets even better. Herbert Benson found out that with just as little as 15 to 20 minutes of meditation a day, you can see a significant change of emotional and physical well-being over time.

Did I convince you yet? If yes, here's a little help on how to start:

1. Look for a space where you won't be disturbed, and just be in silence for 15 to 20 minutes. (Start with 5 minutes if you want) Make it a ritual. It's beneficial to practice in the same spot and at the same time every day.
2. Before you start, use the power of affirmations to get yourself in a relaxed state by saying for example, "I'm now focused and calm."
3. Set your alarm clock for twenty minutes so that you are not worried about when to stop your meditation, and are fully able to concentrate.
4. Sit or lie down and shut your eyes. You can also leave your eyes open and focus on one point in the room or on nature if you are sitting facing a window.
5. While focusing, concentrate on your breath, and start relaxing.
6. When your mind wanders, let it wander. Don't resist. See your thoughts passing by like clouds in the blue sky.

Mindfulness: be here now

Everybody talks about it, a lot people do it as well. So how does it really work?
Being mindful is being fully present. Being in the now. Being aware that we are alive. Being aware of our emotions without judging them. Giving

us permission to feel these emotions. Although we are always in the present moment, most of the time we are not aware of it. We walk in the woods, but our mind is in office. We eat, but we read the newspaper. Mindful walking would be to be aware of the trees, the sounds around us, the animal noises. Mindful eating would be to fully savour the taste and texture of our meal, chewing slowly, feeling how the food dissolves in our mouth, only concentrating on that, and nothing else.

Mindfulness is the awareness and acceptance of internal and external stimuli. You can feel every emotion in the body. As soon as a painful emotion starts, you can go immediately to its physical manifestation. The purpose of this is to become aware of the physical manifestation of the emotion and accept it for what it is. You connect with the present moment by concentrating on your emotions, or your breath.

Mindfulness works because it creates an alternative neural pathway. Instead of trying to fix something, accepting and observing it become the new alternative. If you feel stressed, observe what's happening to your body. What's the physical manifestation of it? Where do you feel it in your body and how do you feel it?

During the first level, you practice mindfulness by becoming aware of your body and your surroundings and as in all meditations, the practice is losing focus and coming back again. You can also practice it by reframing. Instead of feeling the stress before an important speech or presentation, you can see it as a wonderful opportunity.

Mindfulness changes our focus from DOING to BEING. The constant obsession of "How can I fix it?" very often is counterproductive when dealing with mental/psychological problems. The constant living in the future keeps you from being happy in the moment.

Here's one of the best exercises I learnt from my NLP Trainer Anna Flores.

The least it will do for you – if done regularly – is sharpen your senses, but don't be surprised if it does even greater things for you. For me and some other trainees, it has done amazing things.

The basics of this exercise are centred on seeing (visuals), hearing (auditive), and feeling (kinestetic). The idea is to be "in the moment" and more aware of what you see, hear, and feel.

So you start with being consciously aware of 5 things you see, 5 things you hear, and 5 things you feel. Then 4 things you see, 4 things you hear, 4 things you feel, then 3, then 2, and then finally 1.

You can do this anywhere!
I did this one on a train a couple of years ago: Here we go!

5)
I see a red scarf
I see a black bike
I see a blue sweater
I see a red bag
I see a white cable
I hear voices
I hear a tone
I hear a voice
I hear something scratching
I hear a door
I feel my feet on the floor
I feel some cold air on my hands
I feel cold air on my feet
I feel somebody stepping on my toe
I feel my jeans on my skin

4)
I see a blue and white bag
I see a black bike
I see a black jacket

I see a white cable
I hear a cough
I hear voices
I hear a tone
I hear people moving
I feel my feet on the floor
I feel my jacket on the skin
I feel my feet on the floor
I feel my jeans on the skin

3)
I see a red bag
I see a red jacket
I see the sea
I hear distant voices
I hear somebody move
I hear distant voices
I feel my feet in my shoes
I feel my mobile in my hand
I feel air

2)
I see a red scarf
I see a beige jacket
I hear a beeping
I hear a distant voice
I feel my feet on the floor
I feel my jeans on my skin

1)
I see a red handle
I hear the noise of the train
I feel my back against the chair

Do this five times a day for 3 weeks and let me know what it did for
you!

Breathe right and conquer

As I mentioned before, the easiest way of meditation is breathing. It's something all meditation techniques have in common and it's an easy thing to introduce in your life even if you don't meditate for 15 or 45 minutes a day.

One result of our stressed and fast-paced world is that our breathing becomes shallow. The result of shallow breathing is even more stress and anxiety. The result of even more stress and anxiety is that we go into the so-called "fight or flight" response. And that's how we live most of our days. Fortunately we can reverse this. Because our mind and body are connected and we know that calm and well-being leads to deep breathing, this means that deep breathing in turn leads to calm and well-being.

Herbert Benson found out that we can reverse the "fight and flight" response and enter what he calls the "relaxation response" with as little as three deep breaths. Three deep breaths! That's something all of us can do.

You can do a deep breath when you leave home, when you arrive at work, just before work or class starts, just after work or class ends, just when you wake up in the morning, or as the last thing you do before going to bed. I do it every time I get to a red light or when I'm in the line of the super market. Three deep breaths at strategic points through the day can transform your life.

The Importance of Sleep

Before Edison invented the light bulb, the average sleep hours were 10 hours per night. Today, the average person gets about 6.9 hours of sleep during the week, and 7.5 hours on the weekend. Who still gets a full eight hours of sleep? In the US, on average only 25% of the people between 18 and 29 years still get a full eight hours of sleep.

We have to look at sleep as an investment and make it a priority.

Sleep is so important. It strengthens the physical immune system significantly and raises energy levels. But it's a personal thing. You have to find out how many hours of sleep you need.

Some of the disadvantages of lack of sleep are putting on weight and impaired motor skills. There are 100,000 road accidents on average each year as a result of lack of sleep, which results in 40,000 injuries and 1,500 deaths on US streets. The same happens at work. Workplace accidents because of lack of sleep cost companies 100 billion USD a year.

Further, lack of sleep hurts our creativity, productivity, and memory. A big mistake I made when I used to study was to tell myself "Let me stay up two more hours to study" It's scientifically proven that I could have done a lot more studying if I went to bed early. If you sleep enough, you remember the material better, and you are far more creative.

When we don't have enough sleep, we get cranky, irritated, and anxious. Lack of sleep can lead to moodiness, and in the worst case depression But it's not only the physiological effects of sleep. Sleep also has a psychological function. At night, our mind processes a lot of the things we have gone through throughout the day, and many times, it resolves unresolved issues. This is why when you go to sleep with a problem you often wake up with the solution. If you don't give yourself the opportunity to "complete" your dreaming, complete your problem-solving through the night, you wake up with that problem unresolved. This happens whether you are aware of it to not. Over time, this can mount up to a lot of unresolved issues, and we are more likely to enter depression when those are suppressed.

Physical and Psychological need of sleep

Sleep more or less eight hours a day. For me, six hours plus a one and a half hour nap works best. Power naps have been proven to be very efficient. Take your internal rhythms into account. How many hours do YOU need, are you a night person or a morning person? What's right for you?

If you have problems falling a sleep because you eat too late or exercise too late, give yourself the permission to be human. You could tell yourself "Well this is an opportunity to think and reflect." When I experience jet lag while travelling to the US from Europe, I usually wake up at 5 AM, I think "Great, 5 AM is a great time get to work any way". I get up and start working instead of rolling around not being able to sleep any more anyway.

William Dement from Stanford has studied and documented the effects of sleep deprivation on well-being. He found that cognitive skills and physical performance are impaired by sleep deprivation, but mood is affected even more. People who get less than a full night of sleep have a tendency to feel less happy, more stressed, more physically vulnerable, and subsequently, more mentally and physically exhausted. Sufficient sleep on the other hand makes us feel better, happier, and more active.

Shawn Achor talks about an incredible experiment: People who sleep 8 hours can remember 70% to 80% of positive and negative words they memorized before sleeping. People who memorized the same set of words and only slept 5 hours still remember about 70% of the negative words, but only 20% to 30% of positive words.

The Importance of Touch

Touch improves everything. It's a physical need like sleep, exercise, and relationships and has the following benefits:

- Touch strengthens our immune system significantly, while a lack thereof weakens it drastically.
- Touch helps overcome injuries.
- Children grow more when they are touched and their cognitive development is affected by touch. (On the other hand mental problems like mood disorders or eating disorders are very often associated lack of touch).
- Touch can help us overcome depression and anxiety.

William Masters & Virginia Johnson - two the most important sex therapists and researchers have shown that most sexual dysfunctions (between 70 and 95 %) can be resolved simply with the help of touch.

Tal Ben Shahar told this incredible story about a hospital ward for "Premature babies":
One of the sections in this ward had a much higher level of success compared to the other sections: The babies were getting better much more promptly, they were healthier and they showed better cognitive and physical development when they followed up with them in the long term.

So they were wondering why that happened. Everything else being identical, they thought it might be the air, or the location within the hospital.

One night, a doctor stayed in the ward, sitting somewhere out of sight when he heard a sound.

A nurse that worked in a hospital for a long time came in. She picked up a premature baby, which was against the rules of the hospital, because it was not allowed to touch the babies or take them out of the incubators. So the nurse picked up the baby and just stroked him very gently, talked to him, and then put the baby down. Walked to the next incubator, picked up the next baby, stroked him gently and put him down. She did this to every baby in the section. She did it late at night during her shift because it was against the rules. That incident brought forward a whole line of research about the importance of touch with babies in general, especially with premature babies.

Tiffany Fields found out that premature babies who were subjected to 45 minutes of massage a day put on 47% more weight during their time in the hospital and showed better development (physically, and in their cognitive and motor skills) one year later.

Harry Hollow examined touch deprivation: He took monkeys away from their mothers. These monkeys got everything except touch. The result was that the monkeys didn't grow as much, their cognitive development was impaired and they even displayed autistic behavior.

A cruel real life example is what former Romanian dictator Ceaucescu did. He took away a lot of children from their parents, especially if their parents were dissidents. 150,000 kids were raised in homes. These kids were around 3-10% smaller, way below IQ 100, their motor development was impaired significantly, and they showed signs of autism.

Touch is so important…and so are hugs!
Psychologist Virginia Satir states: "We need 4 hugs a day for survival, we need 8 hugs a day for maintenance, we need 12 hugs a day for growth" and Jane Clipman found out that if we give at least 5 (nonsexual) hugs a day, after 4 weeks, our happiness level goes up significantly.

Smile like your life depends on it

Smile! Even if you don't feel like it! Buddhist monk Thích Nhất Hanh knew all along what science found out recently: "Sometimes your joy is the source of your smile, but sometimes your smile can be the source of your joy".

Smiling improves the quality of your life, health, and relationships. Science has demonstrated that laughing or smiling a lot daily improves your mental state and your creativity. It tricks your brain into thinking that you are happy, so it starts producing the neurochemicals that actually do make you happy.
Some of the benefits of smiling are the following:

• It releases serotonin (makes us feel good).
• It releases endorphins (lowers pain).
• It lowers blood pressure.

- It increases clarity.
- It boosts the functioning of your immune system.
- It provides a more positive outlook on life (Try being a pessimist while you smile).

I agree: Authentic positivity is always better than a fake one, but there is significant evidence that changing your behaviour first – facial expression and posture – can dictate emotional change.

A study by Tara Kraft and Sarah Pressman at the University of Kansas demonstrated that smiling can also alter your stress response in difficult situations. The study showed that it can slow your heart rate down and decrease stress levels – even if you are not feeling happy. Smiling sends a signal to your brain that things are all right. A study by Wayne University on smiling has even found a link between smiling and longevity!

If you think you have no reason at all to smile, hold a pen or a chopstick with your teeth. It simulates a smile and might produce the same effects.

When you smile, your entire body sends out the message "Life is great" to the world. Studies show that smiling people are perceived as more confident and more likely to be trusted. People just feel good around them.

To conclude this chapter, here's once again the best psychological description you'll ever get:

- At least 4 x 30 minutes a week of physical exercise
- Mindfulness meditation – if its' good for you – every day for 10-15 minutes (The very least a few deep breaths strategically placed throughout the day)
- 8 hours of sleep a night
- At least 5, ideally 12, hugs a day
- Smile a lot!   :-)
Go for it!

13. What now?

I hope I convinced you by know that YOU are in charge of your happiness. It's not easy, and you have to train a lot, but applying some of the exercises from this book, you can change your life a lot.

Remember that your life depends on the quality of the questions you ask and those questions will very often determine the direction you take. Remember to ask positive questions like "What is good about …?", "What is going well?". If you only ask negative questions, you won't see the opportunities.

Your beliefs create your reality. To great extent how you perceive reality is what actually comes true. Do you remember the two things that distinguish the extraordinary successful from the rest?
  1. They always ask questions, always want to learn.
  2. They believe in themselves.

You improve your belief by taking little risks, by putting yourself on the line, by coping instead of avoiding, and by showing yourself that you can do it by using the power of visualization.

Make failure your friend, because it's inevitable. There is no way around it, and there is no other way to learn. Learn to fail or fail to learn. Try, try, try, try, and then try once more. Remember that the most extraordinary personalities in our world are also the ones who fail most.

Accept your emotions. There are only two kinds of people that don't experience painful emotions – psychopaths and dead people. So if you are sad or angry remember the most important thing: You are alive, and you are not a psychopath.

I warned you at the beginning. After finishing this book and even doing all the exercises you'll not experience a constant high. Nobody experiences a constant high. Life will still be a rollercoaster. You'll continue having these ups and downs. Maybe not as often, and you will probably recover a lot quicker from the downs. When you feel a painful emotion, don't fight against it. Accept it. Accept it like you would accept a rainy day or like you accept the law of gravity. Say to yourself "Ok. I'm human. This really hurts. It's not comfortable at all. I wish it were different, but I accept it".

Have a journal. Journaling works. When we share and open up, we can make sense of the experiences of our lives and enjoy higher levels of happiness.

Make gratitude a part of your life! Gratitude for me made the difference between selling 30 books a month and selling 50 a day. The more grateful you are, the more things to be grateful for will come into your life. When you appreciate the good in your life, the good grows. Unfortunately, the opposite is also true.

Simplify! Many people wonder why they are not happy although they have all the things that they want in their lives. Why? Because there can be too much of a good thing. Start cutting activities, and start saying no to people and experiences.

Take care and cultivate your relationships. They are the number one predictor of your future well-being. They matter more than anything else in the world. More than an exam and even more than how successful and admired we are. Remember that experiences can give you a spike, a high, but then you'll go back to the base level, like the professors, the lottery winners, and the highly successful individuals who thought they had made it.

Take care of your mind and your body. Remember that exercising is like taking an anti-depressant.

Take Tal Ben Shahar's wonder drug:
• Exercise 4 times a week for at least 30 minutes
• Meditation/breathe deeply
• Sleep 8 hours a day
• Touch (hug/embrace)
Remember the two types of change: The temporary high and then going back to the base level on one hand and the continuous growth on the other. The only difference between them is whether or not you introduce

behavioral changes. The only and most important question will be: What you are going to do differently from now on? Produce behavioral change NOW. This is the core of all changes.

Keep studying. Keep reading. What you learned in this book is only the beginning. Remember the Carlton's study: Those who succeed the most and those who are the happiest are the ones who are lifelong learners, always asking questions, always wanting to know more.

Remember that good intentions are not enough. You have to act and apply your knowledge.

The Power of one! Happiness is contagious. If you want a happier world, start with yourself and infect everybody around you with your happiness. Take care of yourself! First, help yourself before you help others!

If you include only these five exercises in your daily routine, your life will never be the same:
• Write down three things that you are grateful for
• Write in you journal
• Exercise at least 3 x 30 minutes a week
• Meditate
• Do at least one random act of kindness every day.

I wish you all the best and would be happy to hear your feedback. You can send your e-mails or questions to marc@marcreklau.com. I love the feedback from my readers. It helps me to improve my books and find ideas for new books.

If you liked this book, please take a minute or two and leave a comment on Amazon. This will help other readers find the book and spread the message.

Thank you!
Marc

About the Author

Marc Reklau (Esslingen am Neckar, Germany, 1973) is a bestselling author, motivational speaker, and personal development expert.

Marc's mission is to empower people to create the life they want and to give them the resources and tools to make it happen. He still spends at least 20 hours every week researching, studying, and applying the principles and secrets of success and happiness.

His message is simple: A lot of people want to change things in their lives, but few are willing to do a simple set of exercises constantly over a period of time. You can plan and create success and happiness in your life by installing habits that support you on the way to your goal.

His first book "30 Days – Change your habits, change your life" became an Amazon Bestseller "over night" (after one year of hard work). After having 40,000 downloads in 72 hours, it hit Amazon's paid Bestseller lists in its category in seven Kindle stores worldwide—where it has stayed ever since.

It has a combined sale and download figure of over 170,000 copies and has been translated into Spanish, German, Korean, Japanese, Portuguese, Chinese, Afrikaans, Indonesian, Thai, and Italian.

If you want to hire Marc as trainer speaker for your event, you can directly contact him on his homepage www.goodhabitsacademy.com where you will also find more information about him and his work.

I Need Your Help

If you have been inspired by DESTINATION HAPPINESS and want to help others to reach their goals and improve their lives, here are some action steps you can take immediately to make a positive difference:

Gift *DESTINATION HAPPINESS* to friends, family, colleagues and even strangers so that they can also learn about the power of happiness as multiplier or personal and professional success.

Please share your thoughts about this book on Twitter, Facebook and Instagram or write a book review. It helps other people to find DESTINATION HAPPINESS.

If you own a business or if you are a manager - or even if you're not - gift some copies to your team or employees and improve the productivity of your company. Contact me at marc@marcreklau.com. I'll give you a 30% discount on bulk orders.

If you have a Podcast or know somebody that has one ask them to interview me. I'm always happy to spread the message of DESTINATION HAPPINESS and help people improve their lives. You can also ask you local newspaper, radio station, or online media outlets to interview me :)

Bring the simple exercises of DESTINATION HAPPINESS to your Organization

Help each member of your organization to succeed.

DESTINATION HAPPINESS is available at a special price on bulk orders for businesses, universities, schools, governments, NGOs, and community groups.

It's the ideal gift to inspire your friends, colleagues and team members to reach their fullest potential and make real, sustainable changes.

Contact marc@marcreklau.com

To book a presentation based on DESTINATION HAPPINESS or my #1 bestselling book *30 DAYS - Change your habits, change your life* contact me with an e-mail to marc@marcreklau.com

Other Books From Marc You Might like

30 Days - Change your habits, change your life

Contains the best strategies to help you to create the life you want. The book is based on science, neuroscience, positive psychology, and real-life examples, and contains the best exercises to quickly create momentum towards a happier, healthier, and wealthier life.

Thirty days can really make a difference if you do things consistently and develop new habits!

More than 170,000 combined sales and downloads since March 2015.

From Jobless to Amazon Bestseller

From Jobless to Amazon Bestseller shows you the simple, step-by-step system that author Marc Reklau used to write, self-publish, market, and promote his book to over 170,000 combined sales and downloads on Amazon.

The Productivity Revolution

The Productivity Revolution shows the best strategies to double productivity. You'll learn how to dramatically increase your productivity, how to gain an extra hour a day to do the things you love, and how to finally stop feeling overworked and overwhelmed.

18952415R00091

Made in the USA
Middletown, DE
02 December 2018